UNDERSTANDING CHINA THROUGH CARTOONS

A current review illustrated by cartoons from **People's Daily**, Beijing,
with interpretations gleaned from **China Daily**, Beijing.

C.E. BLED

Prepared under the auspices of the Institute for International Development and Co-operation,
University of Ottawa

Published with the financial support of the Public Participation Programme of the
Canadian International Development Agency

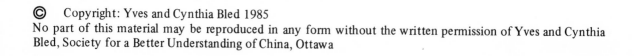

UNDERSTANDING CHINA THROUGH CARTOONS

"We do not wish to hide our errors and defects.
We make them public, because we have faith and
strength to correct them in a set time."
China Daily, editorial, 19 Oct. 1982

Beijing Review*, 2 March 1981

— *Liu Qingtao*

French edition: Y.M Bled, **La Chine à travers les caricatures**, Society for a Better Understanding of China, Ottawa, 1985.

* Beijing, formerly Peking

CONTENTS

PART I: GENERAL SURVEY

PART II: THE MODERNIZATION PROCESS: PROBLEMS

ACKNOWLEDGEMENTS

Acknowledgement is hereby given to the Canadian International Development Agency which provided basic funding for this project through its Public Participation Programme. Also, to the Institute for International Development and Cooperation, University of Ottawa, under whose aegis the work has been undertaken.

The English version of this book has been prepared jointly with the French edition during the sabbatical leave granted to Cynthia E. Bled from the Department of Economics, Algonquin College of Applied Arts and Technology. Thanks are hereby expressed to the College. In addition, the following by their support have contributed through this project to a new dimension for a better understanding of China while attesting to the communicative potential of cartoons:
- People's Daily, Beijing, which supplied the cartoons;
- The Embassy of China, Ottawa, and the Chinese People's Association for Friendship with Foreign Countries, Beijing, which provided reference material for background information to the cartoons;
- The National Film Board of Canada, Ottawa Office, which gave technical advice;
- The National Museums of Canada, for translation services;
- Jane Jin, translator of over 900 cartoons from Chinese to English;
- The Visiting Scholars from China who provided contextual interpretation, especially:
  Li Shengheng, general consultation (French)
  Zhang Gou-zhu, general consultation (English)
- Courtney Bond and Dr. Frederik De Vos for editorial services;
- Merle Storey who steered the book through all its stages providing encouragement and editorial services;
- Martine Pradeau, for translation and editorial services;
- Members of the Society for a Better Understanding of China who provided help and advice in a variety of areas.

Thanks are also expressed to CP Air, Eastern Provincial Airways, The Globe and Mail, K.G. Campbell Corporation in Ottawa, and The Frame Shop of Ottawa which have contributed to the travelling exhibition of the cartoons reproduced in this book. We are grateful to the many other persons who have helped us both with the book and the exhibition, but would single out Rowena T'O Tolson for her considerable devotion to the realisation of the exhibition.

Working across distinctly different cultures has forced us to exercise much personal discretion. We have drawn on information gleaned at the meetings of the Society for a Better Understanding of China over the past ten years where a wide range of "China experts" and others who have lived in China have willingly shared their experiences and insights with the many of us who have made monthly mental trips to China. To all these participants — our thanks. We hope that this look at China through issues raised by the Chinese themselves will succeed in adding another perspective to their presentations.

We accept full responsibility for the content and presentation of the material in this book.

Yves M. and Cynthia E. Bled
Society for a Better Understanding of China
Ottawa, 1985

NOTES ON SOURCES

Chinese periodicals are the main source of reference for this book. In particular:

China Daily, supplemented by **Beijing Review, Chinese Youth Bulletin, China Reconstructs** and **Women of China**.

The following have also been cited:

The Globe and Mail

UNESCO Courrier

Yu, Anthony, trans. and ed., **Journey to the West (Hsi-yu-chi)**, Chicago, Univ. of Chicago Press, 4 vols, 1977-1983. (Alternate reference: Wu, Cheng En, **Journey to the West**, trans. by W.J.F. Jenner, Beijing, Foreign Language Press, 1982)

Bandes dessinées chinoises, Paris, Edition du Centre de Création Industrielle, Centre Georges Pompidou et du Centre de recherche de l'Université de Paris VIII, 1982.

Dawson, Raymond, ed. **The Legacy of China**, London, Oxford University Press, 1964.

PREFACE

The 356 cartoons in this book are mainly from 1982 issues of **People's Daily**, Beijing, one of China's most widely circulated national newspapers. Interpretation of the cartoons is based on information drawn from the foreign-oriented **China Daily** (1983 issues)[1] which emphasizes events and trends in China. Visiting Chinese scholars have also provided significant information.[2]

This study is not intended as another in the countless works presenting western viewpoints on China. Rather it seeks to contribute to an understanding of China within the context of how the Chinese view themselves and their issues. Reliance is therefore placed on Chinese sources for interpretation of the cartoons, irrespective of the extent to which these are critical of the Chinese themselves. The assumption is that these sources, originating from the Chinese government, present information on the working of the Chinese system — both its good and bad points — so that the outside world can better understand the aspirations, problems, and achievements of the Chinese people, and hence the rationale for the actions and pronouncements of their government.

Given the vastness of China in terms of physical, social, cultural and economic diversity, it is impossible to develop a reasonable understanding of the country simply through visits. To supplement such visits by reading western writings is also very subjective since authors often reveal more about their own conditioned perceptions than about in-depth movements in China. Foreigners on extended stay in the country can, at best, relate their limited personal experiences and observations. These cartoons, on the other hand, in the nature of government communication with the general public, provide an overview of day-to-day developments in China as well as an awareness of the physical and human dimensions of the country.

The number of cartoons in each section reflects the priorities of the Chinese during the period covered. Section C on Civilized Pollution, for example, is heavily weighted because the cartoons supplemented a current campaign to eradicate certain practices which the government found unacceptable. Another section which emerges as dominant is that at Part II—J, Personnel and Management. It reflects the government's focus on reorganization in order to accelerate the progress of its modernization programme.

Textual comments have been kept to a minimum, so as to leave the cartoons uncluttered. Additional information is included in the footnotes to help clarify a situation. As supplemental reading, these footnotes are at times longer than the basic text. A few poems have been included to provide an additional dimension. Except where otherwise noted, these are adaptations from Jane Jin's translations.

"Things change ceaselessly," stated Mao Zedung, and by the time **Understanding China** is published, some situations will undoubtedly have changed. However it is our hope that readers will be prepared for such changes by the better understanding of China derived from the book. Development and technical experts working with the Chinese will find it provides useful background material. So will those transacting business in China, sinologists, and tourists. At the same time, the treatment is sufficiently general to appeal to anyone who has even a passing interest in how one quarter of the world's people live today.

---

[1] Footnote and other references to **China Daily**, 1983, throughout the book do not include the name of the paper or year, but only the month and day. Therefore wherever the month and day are given but not the name of the journal or year, reference is to **China Daily**, 1983. A date reference which includes the year but not the name of the journal is to **China Daily** in the year specified.

[2] Cartoons at times reflect a perceived intent which does not correspond exactly to the original intent of the cartoonist. This showed up in differences of interpretations given occasionally by various visiting scholars. However, there is consistency in their conclusions about the impact of the messages.

INTRODUCTION

Cartoons represent sketched humour, often of a satiric nature. They serve as a social mirror as well as a medium to convey perceived and contrived issues in national and international affairs. Where freedom of expression is allowed, the cartoonist becomes a graphic critic of the economic, political and social activities which surround him. Both literate and illiterate people are receptive to the messages they convey, and so insecure and unpopular governments often control their use. In some cases, the cartoonist plays the role of unofficial information agent propagating through his art ideas which the government wishes to convey to the people.

In China original conceptions of cartoons have been found in Han tombs (25–220 A.D.) and were exploited by proponents of Buddhism in the 6th century for inspirational as well as didactic purposes. As a means of social critique, one of the earliest examples was the attack on the administration and police through cartoons and comic strips in the revolutionary newspaper **Cry of the People**, published in Shanghai, 1909.[1]

Periods of national upheaval and revolutionary change have witnessed an explosion in the use of cartoons in China. During the Communist-Nationalist government coalition in 1926, for example, producers of slogans and cartoons were an integral part of the revolutionary army to ensure that all available walls were covered with didactic images and messages through whatever villages and towns they passed.[2]

After the founding of the People's Republic in 1949, cartoons and other forms of art were relied on to contribute to the building of socialism. Scientific and economic progress were highlighted along with the promotion of patriotism and the encouragement of economic effort.

0.1

Unhappy cadre

Cartoon Exhibition

The satirized discomfort of the cadre at 0.1, for example, allows for subtle criticism without rancour.

"It is not art – only for laughs!"

---

[1] **Bandes dessinées chinoises**, Paris, Edition du Centre de Création Industrielle, Centre Georges Pompidou et du Centre de recherche de l'Université de Paris VIII, 1982, p. 9–10.

[2] **Ibid.**, p. 12.

Introduction

Cartoons were used to severely attack cadres[1] of all levels during the Cultural Revolution, 1966 to 1976. With the death of Mao Zedung (1976) and the subsequent overthrow of the Gang of Four,[2] the cartoons widened in scope, continuing to serve as social critic and as a propaganda medium of the government, but also for criticism and reorientation of government programmes and those who execute them.

Four pages of cartoon inserts are carried twice a month in the newspaper, **People's Daily**, Beijing. The paper is a government organ communicating with an increasingly literate population in rural as well as urban areas. Through the cartoons, "new literates" with limited reading capabilities have an opportunity to grasp the sense of dynamism in their country today, the achievements and aspirations, as well as the problems involved, whether of a social or technical nature. Traditional impact of the cartoons has not diminished even with the increasing popularity of television.[3]

---

[1] The term **cadre** is used loosely in China and in this book to refer to all holders of white-collar jobs as well as all persons in positions of authority including peasants.

[2] Led by Chiang Chin (Mme Mao Zedung) who was arrested and subsequently sentenced to life imprisonment for, among other accusations, committing attrocities against thousands of people and for compromising the Chinese Revolution during the Cultural Revolution.

[3] Information from visiting Chinese scholars.

The series of episodes in the life of plants (O.2) is another example of how cartoonists use ideas with which people can relate to convey messages.

O.2

Episodes in the life of plants

O.2a A general concern for plants.[1]
O.2b National unity with plants moving from tropical Canton to Beijing in the north.
O.2c Price-hiking as demand rises with families responding to the tree-planting campaign by buying their own seedlings.[2]
O.2d Family scene. A husband justifies his purchase by saying it is a gift from a friend.

---

[1] Expanses of bare soil exist throughout China as a result of wanton destruction of trees in the past. A variety of tree-planting campaigns have been introduced since the 1950's to counter problems of erosion through wind and water. The campaign underway includes plants for beautification.

[2] This scene is an indication of the new economic order in China today. Prior to 1976 prices were rigidly controlled, and there was no place for bartering.

Many problems encountered by China are revealed in these cartoons. For example, there are:
- the inveterate complainer (O.3);
- and those who do not pull their weight in the development drive but simply follow in others' footsteps (O.4).

O.3

夏天不好冬天好，冬天又想夏天好!

Always complaining

为怨天尤人者画像

Summer is better

Winter is better

蔡振华

O.4

爱循现成脚印的人们

踩人脚印，
跟人屁股。
吃现成饭，
走方便路。

不冒风险，
不致迷途。
平平安安，
舒舒服服。

披荆斩棘，
别人担负；
按步就班，
我行我素。

墓之如画
池北偶诗

不求创新，
但求稳步。
磨磨蹭蹭，
蹒蹒跚跚。

The Followers (O.4)

Stepping in others' footsteps
    following behind.
Reaching for the ready meals
Treading the convenient way.

Never take a risk
    avoid getting lost.
Safe, safe . . . .
Comfortable, comfortable . . . .

Cutting the weeds to pave the road
    that's someone else's business.
Leisurely, step by step
    that's my way.

No innovation.
Sound and safe I am
    grinding slowly . . .
    and hesitantly . . . .

People who only follow others' footsteps

The government of China emphasizes that China is a Communist country but the brand of Communism now practised is different from that of previous years. Chinese writers, for example, when comparing pre-1976 economic policies with those under the current modernization programme, refer to the former as "leftist".

The country is always exploring new ways to achieve and accelerate development within its socialist framework, and the government makes no apology for switching policies and programmes in progress, depending on its evaluation of current practices and future implications.

Some of the contrasts between life in China today and that prior to 1978 are brought out through the use of "Then" and "Now" images at O.5 to O.9.

One aspect of change is in the life-style of the people. Most no longer feel obliged to see work and nation-building as the only purpose of life, an attitude which was reinforced in the philosophy of the Cultural Revolution.

Increasingly, people are caught up in individual pursuits while seeking improvements in the quality of life which would release couples from spending their holidays "washing, ironing, shopping and cooking" and allow more time for friendships and other leisure activities. (Oct. 6)

O.5a

Life in pre-1978 China (Then) was to answer the call to work all dressed up in a "sea of blue". (O.5a)

Bell: call to work

Then: Common characteristics

O.5b

Bell: end of day

共性与个性   姜振民

Now: Individual characteristics

Improved "quality of life" allows each worker an expression of individualism — "style by choice" after work. (O.5b)

Introduction

There is an attempt to de-emphasize indoctrination through slogans, a practice associated with the Cultural Revolution era. (O.6)

O.6 **(a)** *Then: More slogans than action*

(b) *Now: More action than slogans*

The standard of living has improved to a point where urbanites are fussy about the type of food they eat: "Nowadays people are somewhat better off, and it is understandable that they reduce cabbage consumption to include a variety of vegetables in their diet."[1] (Nov. 11)

O.7 **(a)**　　　　**(b)**

People now often patronize restaurants whereas in the past such occasions were rare. (O.7)

Barbecue ducks awaiting clients

Clients awaiting barbecue ducks

---

[1] Manager, City Vegetable Company, Beijing.

16

Politeness and respect for others are promoted by the government and contribute to making eating out a pleasant experience. (O.8)

O.8   (a)   (b)

Then: Macho table manners keep women away

从前吃烤肉必须这姿式，故一般没有女顾客问津。

如今多是由服务员代烤，更方便顾客就餐了。

Now: Served by waiters

Families can now spend leisure hours at the zoo observing an increasing variety of animals. Previously only a few animals were found there. (O.9)

O.9   (a)

从前所谓的「万牲园」（动物园），在解放前只，剩下几只驼肉、几只猴。

Then: Few ostriches and monkeys in zoo!

(b)

如今，珍禽、异兽不计其数，每年接待由全国各地来的游人。

狮虎山

Now: All kinds of rare and precious animals from all over the country

Introduction

The cartoons are not always original in conception. Importance is placed on the message rather than on the originality of the art. The intent is basically to alert, to induce reflection, to correct and to achieve a desired end.

O.10

牧童短笛

At times they are undisguised modifications of past images. (O.10)[1]

O.11

——开 门! *Knock, knock* 江 帆

They might also be adaptations from the foreign press. (O.11)

---

[1] Original version of the cowherd and his flute (minus his transistor) is found in **The Mustard Seed Garden** (1679–1701), reproduced in **UNESCO Courier**, Dec. 1982, p. 16. Variations on this theme turn up in many modern Chinese paintings.

18

PART I
GENERAL SURVEY

A. THE RESPONSIBILITY MOVEMENT

The Responsibility Movement, introduced in 1979, refers to the decentralizing of responsibility in order to accelerate the achievement of China's four modernizations.[1] Under this system, individuals as well as producing units are encouraged to not only meet quotas, but to maximize production in whatever way they can and to personally share in the rewards.

A.1

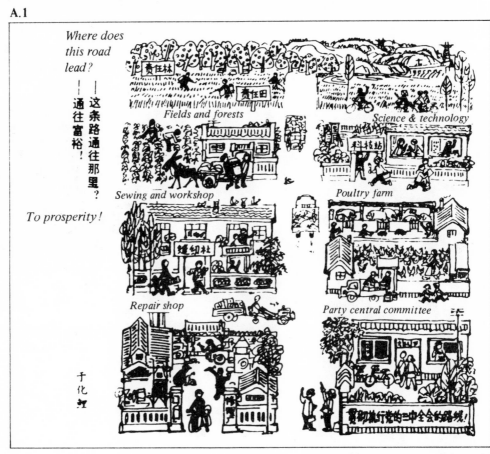

The "road" to prosperity links income and labour so that those who contribute the most will earn the most. (A.1)

Passive egalitarianism whereby some people stand aside and simply share in the productive efforts of others is discouraged under the Responsibility Movement. The aim is to replace this attitude by a pattern of contributory involvement and proportionate compensation.

---

[1] The four modernizations are now defined as science, agriculture, education and technology.

过 秤

These years we all get fat government contracts

The Movement was first introduced and welcomed in the countryside. (A.2)

A.3

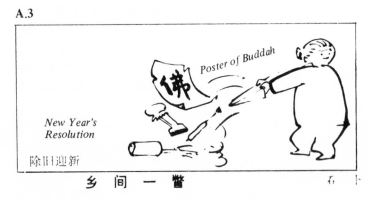

New Year's Resolution

Poster of Buddah

除旧迎新

乡 间 一 瞥

Replacing the old with the new

Peasants were faced with discarding old customs and ideas, and being receptive to new ideas and practices compatible with economic advancement. (A.3)

A.4   *Dared to be rich*

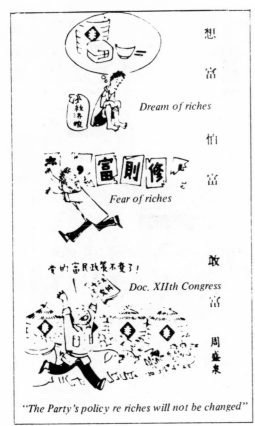

Dream of riches

Fear of riches

Doc. XIIth Congress

"The Party's policy re riches will not be changed"

Because of the harassment which took place during the Cultural Revolution, the government found it necessary to repeatedly assure both peasants and urbanites that there would be no change in the Party policy which encourages hard work and the resulting reward of personal gain.[1] (A.4)

---

[1] A writer in **China Daily** (Dec. 24) puts these fears in perspective thus:

"Not long ago, I heard that a young couple in Guangzhou opened a duck restaurant. They worked hard for three years and earned a profit of 30,000 yuan. Then, suddenly, without prior notice, they shut up shop and announced that they did not intend to reopen. City authorities asked them why, but they said nothing.

Privately, they said to their close friends: "We have earned enough. Let's wash our hands before the Communist Party gets wise to what we're doing."

Again, recently, I heard that there is a large field in the country in Anhui suited to planting safflower, a herb used in traditional medicine. For two years, peasants made a large profit out of safflower, and then this year changed to wheat. They said: "Two years of large profits are quite enough."

It seems there are still doubts about the Party's policy of encouraging people to become prosperous through labour. The young couple in Guangzhou, for instance, thought their 30,000-yuan profit was gained because the Communist Party had not become aware of it. Actually, the opposite is the case: they earned the money because the Party has become wise and wants to correct past mistakes.

"Glorious poverty" and "sinful wealth" were historical errors corrected during the Party's Third Plenum of the 11th Central Committee in 1978. The new policy of encouraging prosperity is being implemented with determination. It is not an expedient measure in any way."

A.5

Star worker

Star family

Star community

越
来
越
好

*Better
and
better*

吴
兴
宏

A model "star" worker under the new system is like the red flower in an ancient Chinese poem which states:

A garden full of spring flowers
cannot enclose them all,
and a red plum flower
will pop its head over the wall.
(A.5)

"Those who become rich first, are like the red plum flower which will soon be followed by others" (Dec. 24). This is the essential premise of the Responsibility Movement. As each worker achieves improved productivity and output, the income of his family rises proportionately. If all workers in a community grasp the opportunities offered by the system and improve their economic status, all families in the community will be better off. The whole community which is the sum of the families will thus reflect the new status. (A.5)

Multiply the experience of one community by all communities in the country, and the whole country stands to benefit from the individual efforts of each worker.

Post–Responsibility Movement scenes

A.6

Everybody better off now

The Responsibility Movement is an umbrella one embracing all national minorities.[1] (A.6)

A.7

New Year's wishes

Peasants have thrived through in-increased productivity as well as encouragement of sideline occupations.[2] A peasant, for example, who in 1979 borrowed money "to make a start" could discard his rags and return in 1983 "bearing gifts." (A.7)

China Daily explains the happiness of peasants thus: "They have regained the power of decision over the major aspects of their lives with the Responsibility Movement. They can now decide how to use the land, how to allocate their work, how to arrange their days. They have become, in effect, 'masters of the land'." (Nov. 30)

---

[1] There are approximately 51 national minorities across the country. These enjoy full equality with the majority and dominant Han group.

[2] Sideline occupations might be collectively or privately conducted and include operations in handicrafts, transportation, construction, retail sales, food and service trades. Between 1979 and 1982 output from these businesses increased more than 40 per cent, "surpassing state-owned enterprises." They are encouraged as long as there is no evidence of socialist-defined exploitation such as hiring other than family members for private production. (Oct. 26)

A.8

地在丛中笑

王复羊

Smiling amid abundance

Increased output under the Responsibility Movement. (A.8)

The productive initiative released under the Responsibility Movement is tempered by a number of problems which have emerged, many of which are mentioned in this book.[1] The Movement is likened to the excitement which surrounds the reception of a new bride in the family. "When she comes across the threshold, everyone is happy. From mother-in-law to the youngest sister-in-law, everyone sings her praises. Only a few days later, however, and conflict has begun to appear . . . . There are problems which the new bride has brought in her wake." (Nov. 30)

The government has responded to the problems by open condemnation combined with increased ideological guidance. (Nov.30) At the same time, the advances associated with the Movement outweigh the disadvantages, and steps are being taken to introduce the concept at all levels of productive activity across the country.

---

[1] It should be noted that these problems have not arisen specifically because of the Movement, but are more in evidence because the decentralized authority which the system entails allows more scope for their overt exercise. See, for example, Sections C. Civilized Pollution, E. Housing, J. Personnel, and K. Selected Economic Base Issues.

B. VILLAGE LIFE

What you see is what you get!

Look! Our bowls! 请看碗里

Look! Our home! 请看家里

Look! Our barns! 请看仓里

Look! Our savings! 请看我们心里

Increased material comforts and rising standard of living for peasants. (B.1–B.4)

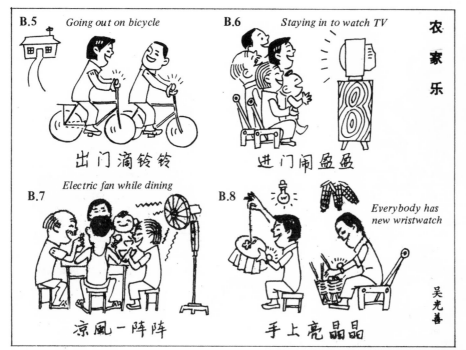

B.5 *Going out on bicycle*

出门滴铃铃

B.6 *Staying in to watch TV*

进门闹盈盈

农家乐

B.7 *Electric fan while dining*

凉风一阵阵

B.8

Everybody has new wristwatch

手上亮晶晶

吴光善

Life in a prosperous Chinese village.
(B.5—B.8)

"Villagers no longer trade only vegetable seeds when visiting. Now they stop to admire one another's chrysanthemums and roses, and wheedle a few cuttings. A new trend for bedtime reading are manuals on flower cultivation."[1] (Nov. 9)

Paper-cuts, once used for window decorations, are replaced by television on the window-sill.[2] (B.9)

B.9

窗　花 *The window plant* 翟军海

---

[1] Mary Sheridan Chen, University of Toronto professor, on extended visit to Jingang Brigade, Sichuan Province, writing in **China Daily**. (Nov. 9)

[2] Ownership of a television is the new status target compared to a watch, sewing-machine or bicycle in pre-1978 China. By June 1984, every peasant household in one brigade in Xuzhou City, Jiangsu Province, had a television (**China Reconstructs**, June 1984, p. 35).

B.10

村姑新扮 *New fashions for country lasses*

Peasants, especially the young, reflect modern style. Uniform bobbed hair or pig-tails and unisex dark coloured pants and tops worn up to 1978 are gradually being phased out. (B.10)

B.11

农村趣闻

张德林

Good news for villagers

Marriages

New barns

Homecoming

缺粮户——新建仓　　　光棍汉——娶新娘　　　外迁户——返故乡

"Vegetable farmers in the suburbs are richer than city workers" and 200 to 300 yuan seem like nothing to them.[1] (July 1) (B.11)

Kunshan County, Jiangsu Province is an example of a rural area with changing life styles. Here the residents now serve soft drinks and tea to visitors instead of plain water as in the past, and in summer they use light sparkling wine. Average annual consumption of household items per 100 persons in the county was estimated in 1983 as follows: 317 cakes toilet soap; 70 bottles cologne; 303 boxes mosquito-repellent incense; 60 bottles insect repellent; 260 packages detergent. (Jul. 12)

---

[1]　Manager, Xisi Furniture Store, the largest in Beijing.

27

B.12

Running water is available in most built-up areas in China today.[1]
(B.12)

战士又来俺家住 *Returning soldier* 李二宝

The search for increased productivity is a continuing one and changes are made when necessary, or established programmes continued.[2]

New approaches to farming are constantly being explored. (B.13)

B.13

小 牛 学 耕   *Calf learning to farm*   周丽泉

---

[1] In the cartoon an appreciative soldier brings water as a gift to an old lady who once provided him with lodging, only to find that the water jar of the past is now used for storing oil.

[2] An example of an expanded programme is the agricultural air fleet, first used in 1951 and now composed of 200 planes. Its effectiveness has been proved and 28 provinces, municipalities and autonomous regions are offered a wide range of services – pasture planting, fertilizer spreading, weeding, pesticide prevention and destruction, and, more recently, cloud seeding and fire detection. (Nov. 1)

B.14

New farming technology books

Literate farmers are now avid readers of agricultural science and technology books.[1] (B.14)

老兵新传　　　　　程新明（农民）

Old soldier learns new tricks

B.15

废寝忘食

Giving up eating and sleeping for educational TV

Educational television programmes are also increasingly popular. (B.15)

---

[1] From 1979 to 1982, 29 publishing houses issued 2,200 titles in these books but have been unable to keep up with the demand. There is also a distribution problem due to the vastness of the market and often the books are sold out before reaching some rural outlets. (Nov. 15)

Due to the high rate of illiteracy in rural areas, all peasants do not benefit equally from the technological information available. The literacy level of well-to-do farmers is greater than that of the average poor farmer. Only 5 per cent of peasant households, for example, subscribe to newspapers and magazines, but those who do are enthusiastic as to the benefits received. (Aug. 10) A peasant in the Shanghai area pointed out that between 1969 and 1979, no single household in his village suscribed to a newspaper. The only paper received belonged to the production team. The peasants all shared in the paper thus: the women to cut shoe patterns, the men to use as cigarette paper. In contrast, half of the circulation of China's newspapers and magazines today is in the communes.

The peasant referred to above cites his own personal experience which is paralleled by thousands of success stories across China since 1978. In 1981 he read in a Shanghai paper that ground beetles were being used for medicinal purposes. He then went to Shanghai to learn how to breed them and afterwards established his own business. In 1982 he earned 2,250 yuan from his enterprise. Prior to 1979, as he explained, he would have been called a "capitalist roadster" for taking such an initiative, "but now peasants are encouraged by the Party's new policies to become prosperous through their work . . ." "Many", he continued, "realize that hard work alone does not necessarily bring about good results. One must also learn science and technology and get information. Newspapers and magazines therefore have become their good friends."
(Nov. 24)

B.16

Double award
  one for 10,000 lbs of grain
  one for 100 chickens raised

". . . now peasants are encouraged by the Party's new policies to become prosperous through their work."[1] (B.16)

---

[1] See p. 21.

B.17 *A new view of the village*

B.17a

鸡 生 蛋

6,000 yuan for my little nest of eggs

B.17b

Pandora's box – thousands of dollars from aquatic produce

农村新景

水产收入万元以上

陈藏子

聚宝盆

Thousands of yuan are earned from the poultry farm and a "Pandora's box" of aquatic produce. (B.17a, B.17b)

Peasants no longer need to depend on the sun to tell the time. Now they "look down" at a watch. (B.17c)

Progress in animal husbandry depicted by a stream of sheep descending from a plateau in the form of a waterfall. (B.17d)

B.17c

Then: Raising head to tell the time

Now: Lowering head

从前看时间抬头
现在看时间低头

B.17d

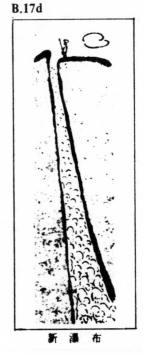

新瀑布

New waterfall of people

B.18

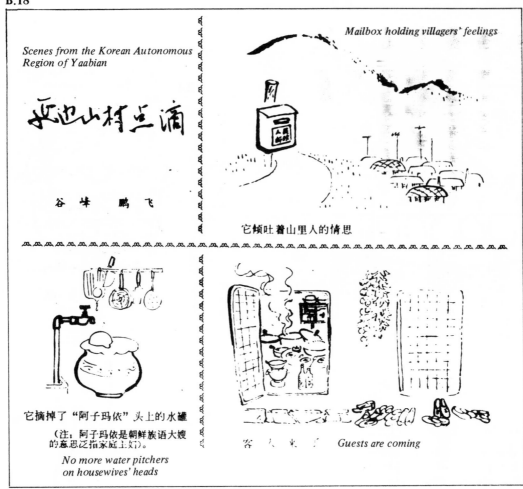

Scenes from the Korean Autonomous
Region of Yaabian

延边山村点滴

谷峰 鹏飞

它摘掉了"阿子玛依"头上的水罐

（注：阿子玛依是朝鲜族语大嫂
的意思泛指家庭主妇）。

*No more water pitchers
on housewives' heads*

Mailbox holding villagers' feelings

它倾吐着山里人的情思

客人来了 *Guests are coming*

Change is evident through all of
rural China, from the autonomous
regions (B.18) to fishing villages
along the coasts.

The extent of change can be seen in a coastal brigade of Fujian Province where, prior to 1956, people lived in small boats at the mouth of the Minjiang River, unable to face the high seas. They were called "crooked toes" because of the disfigurement they developed, being always barefoot on the boats. By 1982, however, the average family income had risen to 10,000 yuan per year. Today the Party Secretary of these former boat people has a 28-room four-storey house with terrace, and many of the brigade members dwell in two to four-storey houses. When the Party Secretary was told jokingly: "You should watch out, you are too rich," his reply was, "The government encourages me to be so." (June 21)[1]

---

[1] Despite assurances from the government, some villagers are uncomfortable with their wealth. See p. 21.

B.19

寄希望于猪年　　　左　川

Advancing in the year of the pig

Affluent urbanites complain of a shortage of lean pork.[1] (B.19)

B.20

王老汉新事　　　曾志巩

Changes at Mr. Wang's

A thankful villager sets up a reading-room which he will share with members of the community.[2] (B.20)

---

[1] The current Five-year Plan includes State support of the agricultural base and provides for the development of improved animal breeds. While studying the animal resources of Tibet, a government commission discovered a thin-skinned tender lean pork-producing strain of pigs which could offer new sources of revenue to the Tibetans while meeting the requirements of city dwellers. (Je. 14)

[2] Many cases are reported where people, especially the elderly, share their newly acquired riches with others. One model contributor, a mutton-broth seller in Kaifeng, Henan Province, gave over 3,000 yuan to public welfare, as a token of gratitude for the opportunity to develop his self-help enterprise. He contributed sets of self-study books and stationery for each juvenile delinquent at Kaifeng reform-through-labour farm; gifts for kindergarten children in his village each June 1; an organ to the factory-run kindergarten for children of Hui national minority; 300 yuan to the local government in a flood-hit area in Sichuan Province in 1981; 300 yuan towards the establishment of a Foundation for Children and Young Pioneers at Kaifeng in 1982; and joined with other members of his family to buy new coats for every childless elderly person in his neighbourhood. (Jul. 13)

B.21

Harvest dance

The lion dance of happiness and prosperity. (B.21)

The Dance is appropriate in the villages of China today but there are a multiplicity of changes — at times questionable ones — which present themselves.

Bumper harvest, for example, create storage problems. In 1983 in Hunan Province, peasants were faced with the following alternatives after a bumber harvest: to sell more than their quota to the State at a lower price; to seek markets in other provinces; to build temporary storage houses or to borrow or rent space; to use individual houses to store part of the grain themselves.

They were counselled to diversify into animal husbandry and grain processing and to shift output the following year to cultivation of barley, corn and beans as means of surplus control. (Oct. 19)

Some peasants now refuse to grow grain. Among them are those who turn to sideline occupations which pay three to four times as much as direct farming. In some areas this "leave-the-farm movement" creates a shortage, but in others it is welcomed as a form of surplus control. It is especially encouraged where those involved contribute to diversification of the rural economy whether through the manufacturing of clothing, commercial services, transportation or other forms of businesses. Some ex-farmers who own equipment, for example, provide services to many who could not afford their own equipment. In addition, an important group of rural middlemen have emerged who by their intervention facilitate the movement of goods from surplus areas to where needed, thus reducing loss when bumper crops occur. (Sept. 5)

B.22

Now then, what have you got to offer me for your diesel oil today?
by Xu Shulin reprinted from Zhongguo Nongmin Bao

Farmers also experience difficulty in buying fertilizer and fuel for motorized equipment due to a lag between demand and productive capacity. At times supplies can be had only through bribes and red-tape, and at prices higher than those set by the state. (Jul. 12) (B.22)

Additional sources of discouragement to farmers are the high taxes and extra burdens imposed such as levies for water conservation, forestry work and broadcasting; pay for brigade and team leaders; funds for road maintenance, education, and also for receptions and entertainment. (Jul. 12)

B.23

A picture of village life at the end of the harvest: quotas are met, produce delivered, and villagers set off on a shopping spree.[1] The day ends at the cinema reserved for the occasion. (B.23)

---

[1] Peasants now go farther and farther for special outings. Shanghai peasants, for example, used to travel one to three hours by train for sightseeing, but now go as far as Beijing to get "a taste of travelling in an air-conditioned bus," as one explained to **China Daily**. (Jul. 19) .

C. CIVILIZED POLLUTION

"Civilized Pollution" reflects a campaign against emerging values and changes in society which China would like to redress and reject. These values are linked to the social consequence of a successful modernization programme introduced in 1978 with the overthrow of the "Gang of Four". The ideal sought is brought out in the scenes of cartoon C.1.

C.1 文明村所见 *Scenes from civilization village* 石 卜

Children infused with a spirit of responsibility follow a "correct" path. (C.1a)

The whole village shows a competitive respect for the teacher who symbolizes their entry into a new era of enlightenment. (C.1b)

A collective responsibility to study ways of changing the standard of living of the people while contributing to the economic advancement of the country. (C.1c)

Each success story is widely publicized to stimulate initiative and enthusiasm. (C.1d)

C.1a / Roadside fruits untouched

C.1b / Respect for teacher

C.1c / Rain does not stop lecture on agriculture

C.1d / Our village is in the newspapers

An increasing focus on materialism which has accompanied the current rise in the standard of living. (C.2)

——我是唯物主义者 *I'm materialistic*

Changed values: the fruit tree branches overhanging the roadside are stripped bare.[1] (C.3)

半 边 灾 翟军海

Half abused

Family relationships reflect the changing economic and social patterns.

Father rich!

Parents adjust to support the new lifestyle of the younger generation. (C.4)

Poor devoted parents

---

[1] Contrast the roadside scene at C.1a where the fruits are left untouched.

A strong condemnation of materia-listic trends in the society.[1] (C.5)

C.5

守
护

胡宏海

The bereaved

---

[1] The scene is all the more striking since China has a tradition of closely-knit family structure with deep respect for elders. However, changes in burial customs have made it easier for the younger generation to place material concerns first and de-emphasize traditional norms.
During the Qin Dynasty (221–207 B.C.), cremation was practised and continued to the 13th century. It was subsequently forbidden until 1911. Large tracts of land were therefore tied up as clan burial sites. To release the land for agriculture and timber, as well as to break with the past, the People's Republic again encouraged cremation in 1949. Simplified funeral rites were introduced to replace the elaborate scenes in the past whereby the "entire family dressed in sackcloth, let the hair go unkempt and wailed. Professional mourners were (also) engaged to lend more volume to the wailing of family members" (Nov. 30). Now that the rites are "reduced to only paying respects to the remains and holding a memorial meeting" (Nov. 30), the emotional impact is minimal and family members turn quickly to inheritance matters.

Civilized Pollution

Cartoons C.6–C.12 reflect a Chinese press reaction to undesirable social attitudes and actions.

文明的污染　池北偶诗　王复羊画

C.6

Indifference

坐　视　不　理

C.7

Littering 孩子的疑问

奶油冰棍甜丝丝，　　　扔进果皮箱子里。
人人都爱买一根吃。　　叔叔年纪比我大，
叔叔剥下冰棍纸，　　　为啥不当好孩子？
随手把它扔在地，　　　难道大人不用讲卫生，
我也剥下冰棍纸，　　　五讲四美只是儿童的事？

妈妈抱娃娃，　　　全神望窗外，
乘车受体罚。　　　眼睛也不眨。
没有位子坐，　　　妇孺头站众，
站得腿发麻。　　　青年都坐下。
叔叔和阿姨，　　　你说不象话，
装聋又做傻。　　　他说没有啥。

Littering (Child's Question) (C.7)

Popsicles! How sweet!
One for each.
Uncle takes your wrap
   tosses on the ground
I too take your wrap
   garbage bin for me!

Uncle is older.
No need to behave?
Is sanitary not for grown-ups?
Five Lectures and
   Four Beautifications – only for
       children!

Indifference (C.6)

Mother with child
   Punishment on bus.
No seat . . . Legs numbed.
Uncles and aunts[2]
   all deaf and feigning stupid.
Gazing out the window
   not one eyelid blinking.

Children, women pay
   to stand
Youth to sit.
"Outrageous" I think.
"Never mind" said he.

---

[1] "Social order," said the Chariman of the National People's Congress, "will soon become as good as in the late 1950s and early 1960s." Severe punishment will be meted out to "gang leaders and hooligans using lethal weapons; those who assault or murder a state functionary, or a citizen who informs against, exposes or arrests an offender; leaders of gangs trafficking in human beings; those who make, deal in or steal firearms or explosives . . .; organizers of reactionary or superstitious secret societies for counter-revolutionary activities; and those luring or forcing a female to engage in prostitution." (Sept. 3)

[2] Children call family acquaintances "aunt" or "uncle" as terms of respect.

C.8

Street Heroes

Street Heroes (C.8)

Narrow encounter
   Bike collision
None to apologize
Fighting words —
   reddened face, swollen neck,
   sharpened tongue, throat out-
            thrust!
You call him "God-damned"
He calls you S.O.B.
More fighting . . . energy
Shout to show your guts!
What a pair of street heroes!

马　路　英　雄

狭路巧相逢，　　　　你骂他混蛋，
两车迎面碰。　　　　他骂你孬种。
彼此不相让，　　　　越吵越起劲，
对骂　大通。　　　　咆哮显威风。
脸红脖子粗，　　　　好一对马路上的英
嘴尖嗓门冲。　　　　　　雄！

C.9

Trespassing

瞧　这　一　家　子

"禁止践踏草地"，　　　哥哥跺脚丫子，
分明竖着牌子。　　　　弟弟练腿腕子。
有人根本不理，　　　　乱跑、乱滚、乱踢，
瞧瞧这一家子。　　　　实在不成样子，
爸爸睡草褥子，　　　　莫非不识汉字，
妈妈坐草垫子，　　　　全是睁眼瞎子！

Trespassing (C.9)

   "No trespassing on the grass"
The sign stated clearly.
Some never pay any attention.
Look at this family:
   Dad lies on the grass;
   Mom sits on the grass;
   Big brother stamping;
   Younger brother exercising.
Running, rolling and kicking —
   Just too much.
Are they illiterate
or all blind with eyes wide open?

Civilized Pollution

C.10

Water Wasting (C.10)

When I turn the faucet on, my chatterbox ups!
From heaven to earth, from north to south,
    I talk and water flows.

"No end to talking?" the earth demands.
From eating to drinking to pleasure seeking.
Really! 1000 tons of water is nothing to waste
    when friends encounter.
No more so than
    10,000 words
    which do not suffice.

Wasted!
That's public property . . . .
    No concern of ours.

Water wasting

水逢知己千吨少

一边拧开水龙头，
一边打开话匣子，
从天南扯到地北，
水哗啦哗啦地流着，
话没完没了地直说。

从吃喝聊到玩乐，
真是水逢知己千吨少，
话语投机万句不嫌多。
浪费的是公家的水，
哥儿们管它干什么！

C.11

敢登攀

古塔修缮，
谢绝参观，
请君止步，
设置栏杆。
男女勇上，
一身是胆，
不顾禁例，
不畏艰难，
争先恐后，
男敢登攀，
行动自由，
蹲无忌惮，
此等游客，
实在可叹。

Climbing dilapidated pagoda

Climbing Dilapidated Pagoda (C.11)

"Pagoda under repairs"
"Please do not enter"
"Slow down — no fence"
Ah! men and women full of guts
    ignoring the prohibition law.
Fearing not the risks
    bravely they fight to climb on.

"I'll do as I wish
What do I care!"

Such tourists! What a pity!

Civilized Pollution

C.12

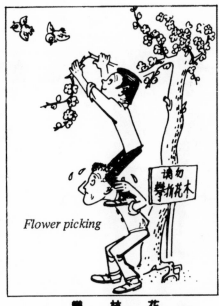

Flower picking

Flower Picking (C.12)

Springtime of multicolours
Lovers' garden trails
Miss not the flowers
Pick while they're there
Don't wait 'til they wither
　　Bare branches to be picked
Never mind the public interest
Never mind the rules.
Fear not the law
Five Lectures and Four Beautifications
Behind me they go.
　　Forget Lui-Fung
　　Go after Latz.[1]

攀　枝　花

万紫千红赏春时，　　　不管公德与法纪，
结伴游园乐滋滋。　　　不怕批评吃官司。
有花堪折直须折，　　　五讲四美抛脑后，
莫持无花空折枝。　　　不学雷锋学拉兹。●

●拉兹是印度影片《流浪者》的主人翁。

---

[1] Lui-Fung (Red Army soldier who also was promoted as model citizen during the 1960s). Latz (Possibly refers to the wanderer and thief, central figure in the Indian film **The Wanderer**, popular in China in the 1950s when India and China had a very close relationship.)

Civilized Pollution

Another press view of "ten social regrettables"[1] presented in classical opera format. (C.13 – C.22)

The Ten-Faced Clown

十 丑 图   蔡振华

C.13 Power thirsty
关卡在手样样有

C.14 Looting
混水摸鱼饱私囊

C.15 瞒上欺下真凶险 Thwarting the subordinate Cheating the superior

C.16 翻云复雨下毒手 Play into his hands

C.17 Grab while you can
雁过拔毛捞一把

C.18 Shut up if not bearing gifts
嘴上无油免开口

C.19 Watch out while doing something evil
推井下石看风色

C.20 Loafing
贪吃懒做世少有

C.21 损人利己犯刑律 Criminally greedy

C.22 Ignorance causes problems
不学无术出纰漏

[1] "Of late," states **China Daily**, "there has been much talk of cultural and ethical pollution. As press reports have demanded, this scourge must be eliminated." (Oct. 22)

C.23

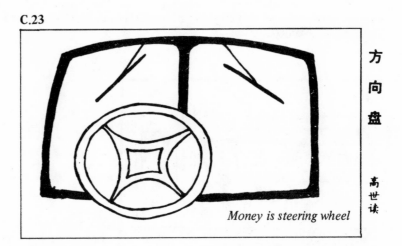

方
向
盘

高
世
读

Money is steering wheel

C.24

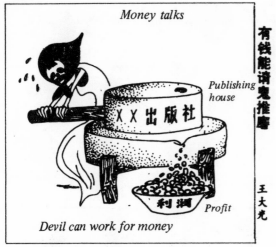

Money talks

有钱能请鬼推磨

XX出版社

Publishing house

王大光

利润 *Profit*

Devil can work for money

The driving force of money. (C.23, C.24)

---

1   Part of this focus on money is attributed to foreign influences. When the Four Modernizations campaign was launched and foreigners welcomed in 1978, the leaders in China underestimated the extent to which social values and cultural patterns would be affected. In the words of Deng Liquin, member of the Secretariat of the Chinese Communist Party's Central Committee and head of the Party's propaganda department, "China followed a policy of opening to the outside world in the past few years. This policy has achieved remarkable successes but also created new problems." (**Beijing Review**, 7 Nov. 1983, pp. 13–14).

45

"People motivated only by money commercialize the socialist spirit. They debase it into a means of serving the selfish interests of individuals and small groups. This is one type of pollution which must be abolished," states **China Daily** (Oct. 22).

C.25

摇 钱 树   景和、景国
Variations of the money tree

All sectors of the population are caught up in the money craze. Professionalism and integrity are sacrificed and, symbolically, artists have no time to create but churn out variations on any theme which will sell. (C.25)

C.26   *The older – the better*

Even the old are forced to yield to money-craving pressure. (C.26)

C.27

Fortune-teller

未卜先知　　西丁

Another problem to be controlled is "feudal superstition" which is "reasserting itself in country areas and even some towns. Witches, sorcerers, fortune-tellers and geomancers are resuming activites." (Oct. 22) (C.27)

At times the unacceptable actions of people are subtle, even to the point of including inaction. "Any type of pollution, however strange and showy, is essentially a manifestation of the ideology of an exploiting class and stands in direct opposition to the communist ideology and social system." (Oct. 22)

A variety of undesirable characteristics. (C.28)

C.28

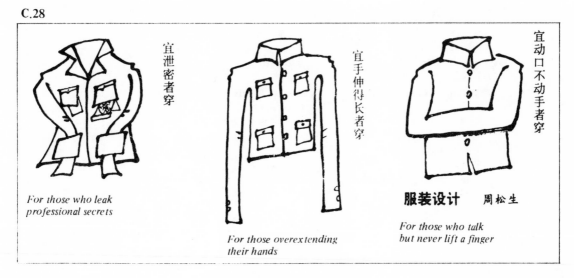

宜泄密者穿

宜手伸得长者穿

宜动口不动手者穿

服装设计　周松生

For those who leak professional secrets

For those overextending their hands

For those who talk but never lift a finger

Clothes designers take heart

C.29

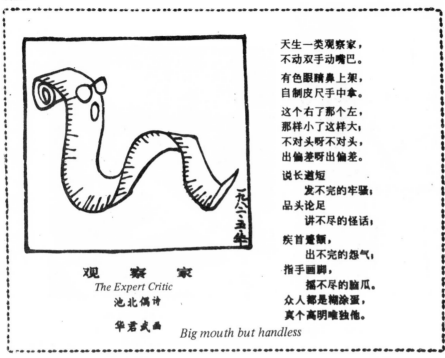

观　察　家
The Expert Critic
池北偶诗

华君武画

Big mouth but handless

天生一类观察家，
不动双手动嘴巴。

有色眼睛鼻上架，
自制皮尺手中拿。

这个右了那个左，
那样小了这样大，
不对头呀不对头，
出偏差呀出偏差。

说长道短
　　发不完的牢骚；
品头论足
　　讲不尽的怪话；

疾首蹙额，
　　出不完的怨气；
指手画脚，
　　摇不尽的脑瓜。
众人都是糊涂蛋，
真个高明唯独他。

The Expert Critic[1] (C.29)

He is
Like some observers who
Move not their hands
　but their mouths.
On the nose are colored
　lenses
Each a ruler for measuring
　others —
　This one is too right,
　That one is too left,
　This one is too small,
　That too large,
　Unacceptable! You have
　　made mistakes.

He criticizes all;
　complains about all.
He comments on everything;
　says nonsense all the time.
He knits his brow;
　is full of bitterness.
A wave of hands to the right
　head always high.
Everyone is an idiot
He only is wise.

---

[1]　Adapted from Li Shengheng's translation of the Chinese.

Chinese Premier Deng Xiaoping identified "manifestations of a weak sense of the rights and duties of citizens" as a "malady" in social relations.[1]

Civic insensibility. (C.30, C.31)

C.30   *Comradeship*

同志关系

江有生

Li is going to have trouble

C.31

好高骛远——啥了不起! 有这种机会我也会这样做

Theory vs practice   王益生

---

[1]   **Beijing Review**, Oct. 10, 1983.

C.32

听
轩
图

毕
克
官

Loitering as an unacceptable social
practice.[1] (C.32)

Snoring crowd

---

[1] A high proportion of unemployed in China today has given rise to an increase in this overt form of non-participation. See
Section D. The Labour Force.

Manifestations of individualism such as those shown below are among the practices which the government tries to correct through education, criticism and self-criticism.

C.33

Centre stage at the concert at the expense of the team. (C.33)

二主角——看音乐会演出有感   潘 海

Two leading performers   Impressions of the concert

Unwrapped fish on the bus. (C.34)

C.34

——谁说车上挤！我这儿多宽绰   胡凤兰

Who said there is no space? I have!

Standing with dirty shoes on the bench to reach for luggage. (C.35)

C.35

最后的留念   张宝生

The last souvenir

51

C.36

某大学学生食堂观感　　*Student mess hall*　　石松涛

In August 1980, Deng Xiaoping[1] stated that "where necessary, all advanced elements who have revolutionary consciousness should sacrifice their personal interests for those of the state, the collective, and the people . . . (and) should do better in disseminating this noble idea among our people, especially the youth."[2]

An appeal to the youth to reject social chaos resulting from selfishness and to be model citizens. (C.36)

C.37

Mao Zedung also saw the future of China in terms of its youth. "The future belongs to you — China's future belongs to you!" was his appeal to them. For the youth to be properly influenced, adults are required to show consistency between their actions and the communal goals they expound.

An example of contradiction in action versus communal goal.[3] (C.37)

---

[1]　Chairman of the Central Advisory Commission of the Chinese Communist Party.

[2]　**Beijing Review**, Oct. 10, 1983.

[3]　The clerk's interest is focused on the fish, not on the customer. Her insincerity is reinforced by the action of placing the slogan upside down.

C.38

Another example of behavioural contradiction showing inconsistency between the visualization of "understanding" and its application. (C.38)

射 手 *Marksmanship* 文 涓

The ego must be subordinated in order that true understanding, fellowship and communication between people can dominate.

C.39

Failing this subordination, the result is a collision course and disharmony in society. (C.39)

Each his own idea

C.40

一触即发　　　王复羊

Combustion any time

The crowded public transport system[1] is an appropriate subject to reinforce the need for cooperative courtesy. (C.40)

---

[1] A widow in Beijing who opted for early retirement in 1983 cited as one of her reasons "a desire to cease commuting like a sardine can." "For years," she explained, "sometimes the bus was so over-crowded, I could hardly breathe. At last I'm free of the bus!" (Oct. 19)

During an average work week, the Beijing Public Transport Commission carries 7.6 million passengers every 24 hours, 13 per cent more than it did in 1965. In the same period, the bus fleet, already inadequate, increased by only 7.1 per cent. Each morning, 3,000 buses and 1,800 trams "snake through clouds of (3.7 million) bicycles along 137 routes." This slow pace adds to the discomfort of overcrowded conditions and creates frayed nerves. Although each bicycle is estimated to take up the space of six bus passengers, there is still no question of discouraging their use. Instead, transit authorities seek to cope with the traffic by introducing new routes, widening some streets, and promoting staggered hours in some factories. An extension of the subway is considered for the future when funds are available. In the meantime, courtesy and mutual respect are encouraged. (Oct. 19)

C.41

Lack of kindness and understanding in the ice cold heart of the server. (C. 41)

Jade teapot with heart of ice

This attitude is illustrative of an incident at Guangzhou's largest department store which "shocked people throughout the country" some years ago.

An Iranian princess who visited China went to Guangzhou from Beijing especially to shop in the store. She was interested in a certain type of comb made of sandalwood and asked, through an interpreter, to see the selection. She looked at one, then asked to see a second. But the young salesgirl said, "They're all the same!"

When eventually the salesgirl was persuaded to take out more combs, she threw them on the counter with a bang. The princess felt insulted and started to cry. This incident caused the late Premier Zhou Enlai great concern and he issued instructions to all hotels, restaurants and stores to improve service.

Administrative cadres at the store have trained workers "ideologically and technically" since the introduction of the Responsibility Movement in 1978, and this, combined with a successfully administered bonus system has resulted in a "well-mannered and efficient" staff today. Shopping there is "a pleasant experience" where a smiling clerk asks, "What can I do for you?"; or on not finding a pair of pants which fit in a particular colour, tells the customer: "If the article is in stock I'll keep it for you. Please come again in a couple of days." (Nov. 17)

Enterprises are encouraged to follow the Guangzhou model so that polite service will become more widespread.

A national Committee for Promoting Civic Virtues was established in 1982 to "guide activities for promoting:
— the five traditional standards: decorum, courtesy, public health, discipline and morals;
— the four points of beauty: beautification of the mind, language, behaviour and the environment;
— the three loves: the motherland, socialism and the Party."

Ethics months are dedicated to improving standards along these lines. During the Ethics months of February and March 1983, advances were seen in "improved services and the spirit of 'serving the people and being responsible for the people.' "[1]

C.42

The spirit of "Ethics" month. (C.42)

Cured by politeness

---

[1] China Youth, May 1983.

Neighbourhood committees played an important role as a community link in the past, but have gradually lost their significance[1] with the rising standard of living. One consequence of their decline is the deterioration of relationships between neighbours. (C.43)

C.43   *Neighbours*

Last inch of my boundary

---

[1] Unique to China, the neighbourhood committee first appeared in urban areas in 1954 as a voluntary organization "to help maintain order, mediate disputes, and aid the helpless." (Nov. 15)

These committees were once very effective as local control units, but now "the dilemma of a neighbourhood committee trying to provide increased services with dwindling staff has aroused the great concern of the Party and State leaders .... Peng Zhen, Chairman of the National People's Congress, called on the whole society to cooperate with neighbourhood committees." (Nov. 15)

Once revitalized, they would be instrumental in helping reduce target incidences of "civilized pollution".

Up to the early 1970s, cleanliness in both rural and urban areas was easy to achieve for a number of reasons. For example, old people and others unable to perform hard work were required, like everyone else, to participate in some form of communal activity which might be simply keeping particular areas clean. Also, there was little excess material to create litter and the policy then was to recycle all waste. Group pressure also played an important part. These factors no longer apply with the present relaxed system of communal control and the relative affluence which generates excessive waste.

C.44

Another problem which a revitalized neighbourhood committee would help redress, namely that of indiscriminate garbage dumping.[1] (C.44)

愚 公 也 犯 愁   王树忱

Despair of Mr. Never-Give-Up

---

[1] A lingering memory of the history of garbage disposal in China makes people fearful at any signs of garbage accumulation. Up to the end of the Qing Dynasty, i.e., 1911, streets in cities were higher than the houses due to the build-up of garbage. In Beijing, for example, "people entered their rooms as if going down into valleys." Later, up to 1949, garbage piles were set up along city walls, but those unable to pay for the transport simply dumped their garbage in the streets. Garbage heaps eventually grew higher than the city walls. (Nov. 28)

From 1949 to the 1960s, the problem was solved by the establishment of open pits 10 miles from Beijing city centre, these pits supplementing production team compost yards. Most of the pits are now filled or used for fish breeding. Production teams, on the other hand, have come to realize that only 35 per cent of the garbage is organic material, the rest being stove ash, dust or dirt, and they therefore refuse unsorted garbage. (Nov. 28)

"Every day tons of garbage are unloaded in roadside ditches." Shanghai is estimated to produce 4,000 tons of household garbage each day. (June 27) In 1982, Beijing produced 1,94 million tons. Some trucks, at a loss as to what to do with the garbage, unload on open ground without the permission of production teams. A team agreeing to take 10 vehicle loads will get an additional 10 or 20 loads to deal with. The government has reacted by fining drivers, while villagers consistently protest. "You city dwellers," they complain, "think only of your sanitation at our expense. You dump your garbage near our village causing bad smells, flies and mosquitoes." (Nov. 28)

While flattery is a universal phenomenon, the extent to which it is used is culturally influenced. There is an entrenched use in China which is reinforced by a background of historical class structure. A writer in **China Daily** (Oct. 22) clarifies this point under the caption: "Flattery can cover malicious intent." Stating that he had seen the cartoon of a man cutting a crooked tree in another newspaper sometime ago, the writer proceeds with the following explanation:

The crooked tree was chosen because it came in handy as a support. In real life, some cadres prefer crooked men because such people are adept at flattery and toadying. But "hypocrisy is often the cover of malicious intent."

Another story tells how, in the period of the Warring States (475 to 221 B.C.) there was a king called Qi Xuan Wang who loved archery. His bow was not too hard to bend, but all his subordinates pretended to be too weak to use it. Until his dying day, the king believed his arms were stronger than all other men's.

Some of our comrades have the same misconception as this king who lived more than 2,000 years ago. They fall prey to flattery and judge subordinates by the degree of their subservience.

The basic reason why some people like crooked trees is because they are not straight themselves. They cannot handle "big and straight trees," whom they cannot regard as comrades. Talented people often have faith in themselves. They uphold truth, fight erroneous tendencies, and are thus prone to be censured as "high and mighty" or "undisciplined". Thus, crooked trees are chosen for walking sticks.

The crooked tree and flattery are often associated in Chinese literature.[1]

C.45

选　才　　　　　*Take what I want*　　　　李明玉

---

[1] The cartoon also illustrates the selfish abuse and wanton destruction of trees, a problem which the government is redressing through a tree-planting campaign.

There have been several recent films dealing with retired cadres in China, and it has been noted that in each there was an administrative section chief who, "while the cadre is at his post, fawns shamelessly." This situation a writer in **China Daily** (Oct. 23) likened to that of Su Quin during the period of the Warring States (472–221 B.C.). When he returned home unsuccessful and dejected, "his wife did not descend from the loom, his sister-in-law did not cook him any food, and his parents did not talk to him."

But later when Su became a high minister of state, his sister-in-law "crouched on the ground and kowtowed to him repeatedly and loudly." When Su asked her how this great change had come about, she answered: "This is because you are now in a high position and have a lot of gold."

"Playing up" to those above was a norm, if not obligatory, in the old society, and the practice is becoming disturbingly obvious today. (C.46)

C.46

新 "南郭先生"

Modern "Mr. Nankuo" (famous fiddler)

Flattery permeates all levels of the society. Even the Monk Pig who represents fidelity and righteousness in the Chinese classic **Journey to the West,**[1] behaves in the same way as Su's sister-in-law: Looking down with disdain on those below, but shuddering with fear and respect before those above. (C.47)

C.47

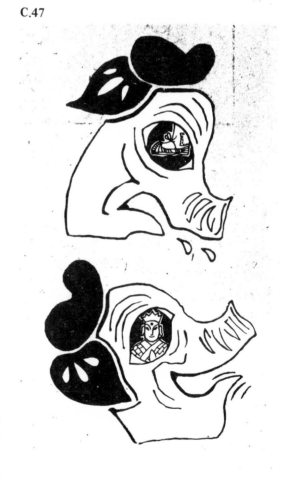

——滚……原来是师父！　王 炬

Get out! Oh its you, my old master

---

[1] 16th century Chinese novel **Hsi-yu-chi,** trans. and ed. by Anthony C. Yu, as **Journey to the West** (Chicago, University of Chicago Press, 1983).

One aim of the "Civilized Pollution" campaign is to reduce criminal elements in the society.

C.48

Pesticide spraying

除
虫

孙
以
增

Criminals are like insects to be eradicated by pesticide spraying. (C.48)

(Insects: criminal elements)

Much of the criminality is linked to unrealized aspirations of the people whose latent desires for material goods have been aroused by the possibilities of affluence which they see others achieving.[1] Gangs have also sprung up who, as young people, were uprooted during the Cultural Revolution and are today displaced, disillusioned and resentful. In addition, there are the unemployed who made up 23 per cent of criminals in 1982.[2]

The government has made a distinction between criminals who can be redeemed through reeducation and 'hardened criminals' — "murderers, robbers, rapists, embezzlers and other law breakers."[3] The latter are subject to severe punishment. "This is vital for maintaining social stability and safeguarding the people's lives and property."[4]

---

[1] Economic crimes are widespread. In 1982, for example, 1.3 million cases of economic profiteering were exposed. Of the 76,200 worst offenders, 13.3 per cent were workers, cadres, and staff members from government offices. Black-marketing of television sets, tape-recorders, computers and foreign currency represented the greatest proportion of cases. (June 29)

[2] **Beijing Review**, September 12, 1983.

[3] **Ibid.**

[4] **Ibid.**

The campaign against crime is run at the same time as one against those "who are apathetic to the negative and currupt phenomena they see frequently." (Oct. 22) All citizens are required to cooperate in reporting anti-social attitudes and crimes against the state. The legend of Wu Song is used to reinforce this point.

C.49

Wu Song beating a tiger

Wu Song had the strength to overcome a tiger.[1] (C.49)

C.50

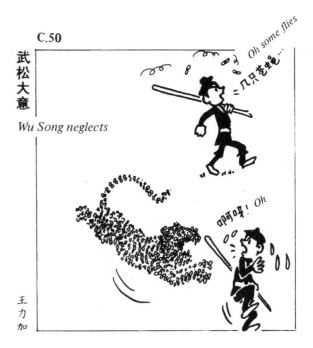

武松大意

Wu Song neglects

王力加

However, he was overwhelmed by a tiger force built up from a few flies (crimes) which he initially ignored as small and insignificant. (C.50)

One explanation in China for the high crime rate[2] is that initial incidences were often ignored and left to build up. In other cases, "some public security and judiciary workers put undue emphasis on educational work and, where severe punishments were needed, favoured leniency. The result was that with nobody around to teach them a lesson, some hardened criminals perpetuated outrages to the great distress of the people around them." (Sept. 12)

---

[1] Woodcut from **Beijing Review**, Oct. 3, 1983.

[2] Seven to nine per 10,000 which is possibly among the lowest in the world, but "too high" from China's point of view. (Sept. 1)

Abuse of historic monuments is one of the anti-social practices singled out for correction.[1] Unless monuments are treated with care, they will eventually be ruined.

C.51

Lack of respect for monuments. (C. 51)

如此"保护" *Preservation of artifacts*

有些文管所的摄影部，竟以文物当布景和道具以招徕顾客 *Artifacts used for tourist attraction*

C.52

Some people's actions are similar to a reversal of roles between the dragon and the phoenix.[2] (C.52)

凤 戏 龙   *Phoenix after dragons*   李时民

---

[1] This policy is contrary to that experienced during the Cultural Revolution when many historic monuments were wantonly destroyed in an effort to denigrate the past. These monuments were seen as reminders of the forced labour of the working class and the many lives lost in their building. Today monuments of the past are seen as examples of the skills and potentials of the Chinese people.

[2] In Chinese folklore the dragon chases the phoenix. Here the phoenix (the young lady) is destroying the mighty dragons (monuments) by her touch.

Civilized Pollution / Alcoholism

Alcoholism is a social vice which should be controlled.[1]

"Intoxicated mums" are harmless (C. 53) but a drunkard can represent social dynamite filled with revenge and suspicion. (C.54)

The addictive effect of alcohol. (C.55)

醉　棍　*Drunkard*　李志平

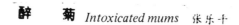

C.53

醉　菊　*Intoxicated mums*　张乐平

条件反射　*Conditioned reflex*

---

[1] The Chinese are proud to state that some communes serve wine instead of water as a mark of their improved standard of living. Neither by religion nor morals are they against the consumption of alcohol, but they are disturbed by its harmful potential.

A faithful husband's solution to the liquor problem. (C.56)

Comment

As the campaign against social evils continues, there is a definite concern on the part of the government lest the movement be seen as a portent of a return to the Cultural Revolution days.

"The ongoing crackdown on serious criminal activity in China has led some people around the world to speculate that this might flare into a political campaign. But the action is, to all intents and purposes, part of the regular work on the agenda of the People's Republic."[1] "... we will not do unto others what they did unto us" during the Cultural Revolution.[2]

---

[1] Beijing Review, Sept. 12, 1983.

[2] Ibid., Nov. 7, 1983.

D. LABOUR FORCE

High unemployment. (D.1)

Too many blossoms – no seeds

头
多
不
结
籽

人浮
于
事

张
乃
株
（太
原）

Jobs are sparse

Estimates vary, but one constant is that under the current modernization drive, unemployment in China has increased to a level considered disturbing.[1]

At present the government considers the situation under control in only one eighth of all the cities in the country.[2]

An estimated 500–600 million jobs will be needed in the next 20 years to accommodate an annual addition to the labour force of 20–30 million. (Oct. 10)

---

[1] From 1949 to 1960 there was little or no unemployment due to the labour-intensive form of production which resulted from a policy of national self-sufficiency as well as from the aim of the government to involve the population at large in the economic-building drive. In 1957, all workers were offered life tenure under the Iron Rice Bowl Policy. A contract system for temporay workers was introduced in 1958 with the Great Leap Forward Programme to accelerate the pace of economic development. However, by 1960 the programme had faltered and 20 million were laid off. From this point on, unemployment as a problem surfaced.

In 1966, under the Cultural Revolution, all temporary workers were made permanent. Those sent to the country-side with the 1960 lay-offs returned to the cities. In all, 13 million workers drifted to the urban areas, but there were no jobs to absorb them. Between 1977 and 1981, 37 million jobs were created, but these were insufficient to stem unemployment. (Nov. 19)

[2] 30 cities. (**Beijing Review**, Sept. 19, 1983)

A shift in policy between 1977 and 1978 resulted in the government deciding in favour of efficiency when faced with a choice between unemployment (or underemployment) and increased efficiency. Rationalization of the state production priorities and resources led to cut-backs and the closing of some operations. (Nov. 10)

Underemployment due to production cut-backs.[1] (D.2, D.3)

D.2 *Too many cows for limited feed*

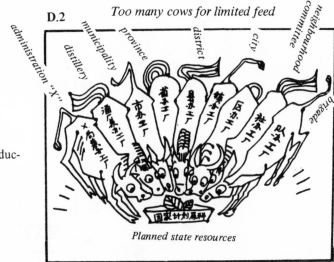

Planned state resources

牛多草少几几饥   万向众

(Cows: factories of indifferent levels)

D.3

好事多磨

Over-enthusiastic

Certain local committees fighting for work

---

[1] An example of this situation is a machine plant in Guangdong which has a workforce of 2,000 but no production quota "for a long time." (Nov. 10)

The contract system[1] is being re-introduced in stages and is expected to reduce underemployment by permitting state enterprises flexibility in employment policies as well as control over work standards. Hiring and firing of workers will be based on competence as well as the requirements of the enterprise.

D.4   众 推 磨 *Everyone pushes!* 吴容芳

Surplus employees. (D.4, D.5)

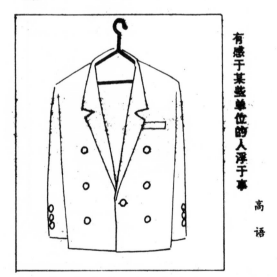

D.5

有感于某些单位的人浮于事

高
语

Surplus buttons (employees)

---

[1] The system had remained in suspension since the Cultural Revolution but in its new format provides for temporary workers to enjoy the same benefits as permanent ones, thus removing one of the criticisms which existed previously. (No. 9)

An experiment in Anyang City which employed 446 contract workers has been hailed as successful. The City offered these workers the same pay as permanent workers starting out in their jobs, and the same incremental scale through the first two years. However, after this period, any increment depended on work efficiency. The contract workers received the same grain rations, medical and labour insurance as others, as well as old age pensions and death benefits. (Oct. 6)

Another version of underemployment. (D.6)

D.6   *Too many switches – one bulb*

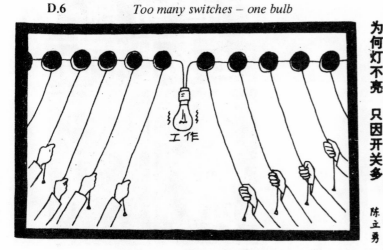

(Bulb is work; switches are people)

Solving the problem of unemployment and underemployment is a phenomenal task.[1]

A cartoonist points out three aspects of this problem:

— establishing wage levels appropriate to the job (D.7a)

— the overwhelming paperwork (D.7b)

— delays in matching applicants' skills with the jobs available (D.7c)[2]

D.7

Diagnosis

---

[1] The situation is akin to a college in Beijing built in 1953 for 100 teachers. There are now 1,200 but only 600 are needed. (Nov. 10)

[2] The task has been compounded by reorganization in educational institutions introduced without consideration for the direct impact on labour placement. For example, separation of the veterinary faculty from the agricultural colleges gave rise to over-specialization so that many graduates could treat hogs and cattle, but not horses, thus limiting their placement possibilites. (Nov. 10)

Labour Force / Apathy and Irresponsibility

Apathy among workers is partly a reflection of personality, partly a relaxation of social controls, and is also due to the Iron Rice Bowl which guarantees a job for life.[1]

D.8   *In-out bulletin*

Versions of apathy. (D.8, D.9)

D.9

多好的草地也有瘦马 *Even on green pastures there is a lean horse* 凤歧

---

[1] The Iron Rice Bowl – "that water-tight guarantee of employment irrespective of efficiency of workers" – combines with the rising standard of living and easier access to modern social distractions to encourage irresponsibility. However, the policy is being phased out. All workers will eventually be evaluated, compensated and retained based essentially on their job performance. (Oct. 6)

D.10

Household work done at office

D.11

没到上班时间　　　徐鹏飞

Not yet working time

Social irresponsibility (D.10, D.11)

The job placement system which has existed up to the present also contributes to a lack of commitment to the job by some workers. Many are assigned jobs in which they have no interest, whether due to the nature of the job or the location. Their prospects for mobility are limited. Even if an opening were found elsewhere, workers could only transfer if granted a release by a current employer.

Disinterest also shows up among those who benefit from automatic placement, i.e., inheriting the jobs of retired or deceased parents. Some parents retire simply so that the children's income can be added to their own pension to increase the family income. There have been complaints in the newspapers to the effect that children of some factory employees have been hired without competition on completion of their military service. (Nov. 19)

D.12

An unfinished chess game

Further examples of irresponsibility
(D.12, D.13)

D.13

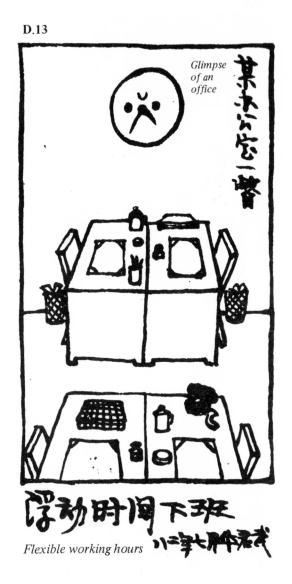

Flexible working hours

D.14

老九！ 不能走　*Number 9 you cannot go!*

While some workers renege on their responsibilities, others end up with an inequitable share of the work. At times the overburdened worker is an "intellectual".[1] (D.14)

---

[1] In 1978, the All-China Science Congress recognized scientists (intellectuals) as part of the working class. (Sept. 3) Before and during the Cultural Revolution, on the other hand, they were at the 9th level of "unacceptables". In 1975 when Den Xiaoping was in charge of the Central Party Committee, he opened the door for the full integration of intellectuals into the society, quoting Mao Zedung who in 1949 pleaded, "Stay with us my 9th brother." Vice-Premier Deng's point was that intellectuals, the "stinking 9th brother" of the Cultural Revolution days, should no longer be excluded. (Sept. 3)

At many research institutes today it has been found that, although intellectuals represent a majority on the staff, only a few have party membership. Measures now taken to facilitate their entry into the Party will allow them to exercise a greater role in policy input — a role reserved for party members.

Honqqu (**Red Flag**), a journal of the Chinese Communist Party Central Committee, has urged the country's intellectuals to be more visible and to help overcome the shortage of trained personnel. Through their different organizations the intellectuals have responded and under their guidance, scientific, technical and consultative services are springing up in the cities, spreading knowledge while providing information to departments where needed. (Nov. 5)

Another modification affecting intellectuals is the introduction of an "open recruitment" system whereby intellectuals as cadres can be selected and transferred among those in office, or recruited from outside a department, through public notices and examinations. These cadres are to be evaluated on the basis of their knowledge rather than their political leanings. (Nov. 3) The mobility allowed under this system contrasts to the lack of freedom which previously existed.

D.15

«Middle-aged intellectuals of our neighbourhood» [1] (D.15)

D.15a

Preparation for class

"Intellectuals are pillars of the nation, just like the workers and peasants .... Middle-aged intellectuals are carrying a heavy social burden but are being repaid with meager salaries and poor living conditions." (Sept. 3)

D.15b

Day off for lecturer, Dept. of Architecture

D.15c

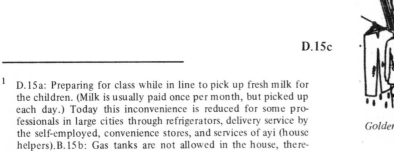

Golden opportunity to catch up on work

---

[1]   D.15a: Preparing for class while in line to pick up fresh milk for the children. (Milk is usually paid once per month, but picked up each day.) Today this inconvenience is reduced for some professionals in large cities through refrigerators, delivery service by the self-employed, convenience stores, and services of ayi (house helpers). B.15b: Gas tanks are not allowed in the house, therefore the day off is used to build a wall.

D.16

我也议价

议价商品专柜
Prices negotiable

粉丝

聘用
150元

Retired worker willing to negotiate his pay.[1] (D.16)

150 yuan – but I am negotiable too!

On the average, women retire at 55 years and men at 60, depending on the type of work done. State employees receive 70 to 80 per cent of their former wage and benefit also from free medical care. Others who cannot support themselves are dependent on their children who are required by law to support them. Childless retirees seek other work if they can, or join the ranks of the poor, dependent on community help.

---

[1] Many retired professionnals give advice, train the young, or engage in a miscellany of tasks such as directing traffic and mediating family disputes. In Shanghai, 2,600 retirees help the police on trafic duty each day. In Northeast China in Harbin Province, over 6,000 work in neighbourhood committees (Nov. 1). Retirees also offer their services in remote places although "some narrow-minded cadres maintain that these retired workers should not get more pay than their pensions. These cadres place restrictions on retired workers going to the countryside." (Dec. 8)

The labour force stands to benefit qualitatively by the rapidly increasing number of young people with higher education.[1] Their ranks are augmented by those already in the labour force who resort to self-study as a passport to progress.

D.17

Some tradition-bound persons are distrustful of the competence of the self-study graduate. (D.17)

闲话桃李

Concerning peaches and plums

自学成才

Self-taught young talents

好吃不了

Too many to be good

安成元

Once qualified but now faced with overcrowding and bleak job prospects, "many outstanding students are giving up city life to go to work on key national construction projects, especially those in the border regions." (Aug. 10) Still, from the government's point of view, not enough are willing to accept these assignments, and "patient work is being done to help them see the need to go where their training is badly wanted." (Aug. 10) In the Northwest and Southwest, for example, there are "thirteen million hectares of unreclaimed land and rich mineral resources representing a golden hill to be opened up by the application of science and technology . . . . There is room for the settlement of hundreds of millions of people." (Nov. 19)

---

[1] Technological advancement, which is being cultivated in China, will absorb a number of the skilled unemployed, but the displacement factor combined with the existing unemployment level portends a problem well into the future. A significant breakthrough will depend on priority programmes in new regions and intensified development schemes in presently backward areas. Special incentives will also be required to encourage free movement to these areas.

E. HOUSING

There is a shortage of both rural and urban housing in China today. This is due partly to a rise in standards and expectations and partly to a policy of low rent and egalitarian allocation, in practice since 1949.[1]

E.1

The gap between supply and demand is such that units are usually allocated before completion. For many people, home ownership remains a remote possibility.[2] (E.1)

Pending distribution bill

Applications

空 中 楼 阁 *Castle in the sky* 赵崇敬

---

[1] Peasants have always been allowed to build their own homes, therefore the problem is less acute in rural areas. As one of the five guarantees of life set out by the Constitution of the People's Republic, housing has been treated as state welfare. Rents have until now been set at symbolic rates, not representing true economic value. The rent on a two-room apartment in 1983, for example, averaged 4 yuan per month. This amount was insufficient to cover maintenance costs which therefore had to be subsidized by the state. (Jan. 21, 1984) The rents are now gradually being adjusted to bring them closer to market value, and over-all subsidies are to be replaced by selective help based on family size, income and housing condition. (June 24)

Another problem is that the average price for units built by the state was 1/3 the cost. Still, only a few people could afford to buy their own homes so the housing situation was not much relieved, while the amount recovered was insufficient to roll over into additional construction. (June 24)

[2] It is estimated that, if each urban family were to get an apartment within the next 20 years, 600 to 900 billion yuan would have to de spent, creating 190 million apartments. (June 24)

E.2 *Magician*

E.3 *Chess game: New housing project*
Players: People short of shelter vs those with special connections

Unfair allocation by cadres contributes to the already inadequate housing supply.[1] (E.2, E.3)

一盘没有下完的棋 *Painstaking decision*

---

[1] Some extreme cases have been revealed where cadres have expropriated or built illegal housing and chosen to dismiss the campaign against such pratices as "passing wind". In Shanxi Province, for example, two high-level cadres were dismissed from office and given one year probation as party members for such behaviour. In the same city, another official defied orders to vacate seven apartments in five different cities, obtained through abuse of power or built with diverted funds for himself and his daughters. (July 29) The Party's Central Disciplinary Commission in Beijing had to intervene to stop the construction of five flats which were being built for the Governor and Vice-Governor of Shanxi Province, and which exceeded government guidelines. (Aug. 23) The province is not unique but typical of selfish attitudes which retard official efforts to provide housing.

There is an active house-building programme,[1] but the government is also encouraging repairs as an alternative to demolition for rebuilding. The Industrial and Commercial Bank of China, which initiated a residential loan programme in 1982, lends funds both for new construction and repairs.

E.4

Many older houses are in disrepair. (E.4)

Older houses seized during the Cultural Revolution are being returned to the original owners and, as a result, the demand for new housing will increase to accommodate those displaced.[2] At the same time, however, funds previously used for maintenance will be released for additional construction. (June 15)

---

[1] Between 1979 and 1982, 12.6 per cent of the state's capital spending went to the housing section. At the municipal level, Shanghai completed a 3.5 million-square-metre housing project in 1983 and immediately started on another 1.4 million-square-metre project in its 1984 programme. This is typical of the pace of building activity. (Oct. 26)

In 1983 Shenyang Municipal Housing Bureau started 300 apartments, each 20 to 25 square metres, with plans for a further 2,000 to be completed in 1984. These were offered at prices ranging from 9,000 to 10,000 yuan. "Prospective tenants, however, put up only one-third of the cost, leaving the balance to be paid by the unit in which they work. Discounts of up to 20 per cent are granted for cash purchases, while a 15-year instalment plan is available for less affluent buyers." Each apartment was furnished with a "double bed, 2 chairs, a desk and a wardrobe." Eighty-seven units were sold in a single day, and the rest purchased in advance before completion. (Feb. 21, 1984)

The Ministry of Urban and Rural Construction Environment Protection recommended the following priority measures to speed up house construction: "Control strictly the size and costs of new apartments. Except in big cities, priority should be given to five- or six-storey buildings, which are the most economical and quick to build. Promote the development of the building materials industry and give it precedence in six respects: in the supply of raw materials, fuel and electric power; in technical renovation; capital construction; loans, both domestic and foreign; importation of new technology; and transport." (June 24)

[2] Approximately 510,000 rooms are to be returned. The Beijing Housing Administration estimates that it will take five years before alternate accommodation can be found for the present occupants so that all the units can then be returned. Once recovered, the owners will be free to rent, sell or occupy them as they wish. (June 15)

F. FAMILY AND SOCIAL STRUCTURE

F.1

Those whose parents are high level cadres, come forward.

Traces of elitism are beginning to reappear. (F.1)

One of the first steps taken by the People's Republic in 1959 was to try to eradicate traces of hierarchical levels entrenched in the social fabric of the country. The over-all aim was to get everyone involved in developing the country with a sense of equality and mutual respect, whatever the task to be done. There was a shuffling of social strata. All persons who through ancestry or intellectual, commercial or administrative pursuits were previously identifiable as members of a privileged class were forced to disown or renounce their past in order to gain full acceptance in the new social order.[1]

Since 1978, some Chinese openly expound an absence of contradiction between class level and commitment to the state. Traces of elitism are beginning to reappear. Kong Dimao, for example, a 77th generation descendant of Confucius, survived the Cultural Revolution and as a member of the revived intellectual class published in 1983 **Anecdotes on Life in the Inner Courtyards of the Kong Family**. This book has been received with fascination in China today. On the other hand, during the excesses of the Cultural Revolution, parts of the Confucian archives held by the Kong family were destroyed. (Jul. 8)

---

[1] All professionals – teachers, doctors, managers, engineers and others in this category – who were not members of the Communist Party were seen as undesirable intellectuals, but allowed to function in their professions depending on the needs of the state, and to the extent that they accommodated themselves to the social changes. During the Cultural Revolution, controlled literature – the only form allowed – condemned these "intellectuals" as "anti-Party, anti-socialist and anti-Mao-thought." They were categorized as "alien, ancient, feudalistic, bourgeois and revisionist." (Sept. 3)

Some members of the older generation are especially concerned that their children marry into the right social class.[1] (F.2)

F.2

子：妈妈，她是我的对象叫……。
母：这我不管，我问她父母是哪一级干部？

苗 地

Son: Mom, this is my girl. Her name is . . .
Mother: I don't care what her name is. What level in the Party do her parents belong to?

---

[1] The average urban Chinese no longer seeks to be identified in the eyes of foreigners, with a peasant or working-class background, as was the case up to the early 1970s. It is now acceptable to acknowledge links with intellectuals, and with upper level cadres. In effect, these niches emerge in Chinese literature as the aspired levels of upward mobility and in which existing members strive to remain.

F.3

The wedding gown, patterned with ancient Chinese coins, symbolizes marriage into wealth.[1] (F.3)

试 "嫁衣"　赵习勤

Fitting the wedding gown

---

[1] Arranged marriages are illegal in China today in contrast to pre-1949, when this was the normal practice. Instances of such arrangements are still occasionally found, but a modified form, which is more common, is the refusal of a family to accept a partner of the "wrong" social standing.

In a case reported in 1983, a university professor and her high-level cadre husband objected to their son's relationship with a middle school teacher on the ground that she was not equal in social status to their son, a university graduate student. All the daughters-in-law in the family were from the best known universities, and the parents feared that a marriage at this level would have a bad influence on the next generation. The parents broke up the relationship, the girl committed suicide, and the son's mother was given a prison sentence for having harassed the girl to death. The public supported the punishment on the premise that young people should be left free to choose their partners without interference from parents or regard for social status. (Jul. 8)

F.4

How could you choose such a job?

Father

Model worker

——孩子，你干吗非要干这一行！

叶春阳

Dedicated young workers do not always receive the unqualified encouragement of "upper-class" parents.[1] (F.4)

     The younger generation in general has resisted both the excesses associated with the social ideals of the Cultural Revolution and the distinctive hierarchical social norms of the past.

---

[1] A generation clash occurs in this cartoon image where the ideals of the young worker conflict with the social aspirations of her father. The disappointed father reacts to her having accepted a job beneath the dignity of the family, while the youth's despair is indicated by the laurels laid aside at her feet. (The high status of the father and his measure of achievement is symbolized by the ancient Chinese coin designs on the sofa handles. His bourgeois standards are reinforced by his western-style dress.)

The press — to the extent that it is free — is in the long run a reflection of popular sentiment.[1]

F.5

In some instances, the resurgence of elitism is a reflection of media promotion. (F.5)

Super star

Star singer

Shining star

Movie star

New star

magazine

人造卫星 *(Media-created stars)* 李时民

In China there is a sort of contradiction in terms in that people expect the elite to exhibit certain forms of distinctive behaviour, while expressing disapproval of such actions. At the same time, the government fears that overt class distinction could lead to general discontent.[2]

---

[1] The press is not and does not pretend to be fully free. Still, until 1978 only government policy was reflected in the press, whereas today it also provides feedback on popular sentiment.

[2] The following is an extract from **China Daily** (Nov. 18) on this topic:
Cadres mix less with the masses
High-ranking government officials mix less with the people than they did 30 years ago, according to a Wuhan newspaper.
A recent edition of News Digest, quoting the Wuhan Wenhua Bao, said some officials now had bodyguards and spent little time with the people, unlike in the late 1940s and 50s when there was no special distinction between the two groups.

The article was written in response to a recent call by a top Party leader for a return to the Party style of the years before and just after Liberation.
To highlight the change in habits, the paper cited a story from the autumn of 1949, when a group of Wuhan officials decided to go to the theatre.
The cadres bought their tickets and watched the Beijing Opera unnoticed. But as they emerged from the theatre one official felt a hand groping in his pocket.
The paper said "pickpockets would find it very difficult to make officials their victims today because they have bodyguards and are no longer easily accessible.

See also footnote p. 154.

F.6

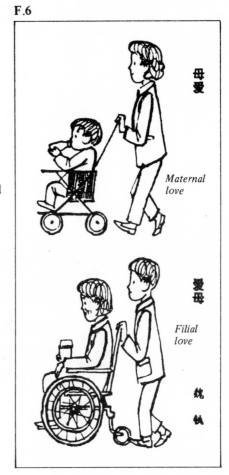

母愛

Maternal love

愛母

Filial love

枕頭

Reaffirmation of filial love and respect. (F.6)

At the establishment of the People's Republic in 1949, the Constitution conferred on women "equality with men in politics, economics, culture, social and family life." (Oct. 5) Prior to this, women had no legal rights of inheritance and were subordinated to the "three obediences — to father before marriage, to husband after marriage, and to son after the death of husband." In addition, they were subjected to four virtues governing their code of behaviour — morality, proper speech, modest manners and diligent work. The woman's place in society was thus clearly defined. Men, on the other hand, were assumed to be responsible and self-policing, and therefore had no similarly imposed code of behaviour. (Nov. 12)

The government continues to promote the unqualified acceptance of women in the face of resistance by conservative elements.

In 1949 women entered the labour force as equal partners. They undertook every aspect of hard work and in compensation were given the right to equal pay, special privileges during pregnancy and breast-feeding, and nurseries for the children once weaned. These rights are, however, at times denied.

The women's section of the General Trade Union of one province, for example, intervened to stop discrimination against women in that province. In some cases women were forced to take up to two years maternity leave with pay ranging from 30 to 50 per cent of income, and at times without pay, whereas current (1983) maternity pay legally average 70 per cent of income. Some enterprises even closed the day nurseries to save funds, indifferent to the dilemma this created for young mothers. (Jul. 12)

My family tree: Mom was born the year of the cow; Dad the year of the rabbit; Brother the year of the rooster; I the year of the mouse. Mother is therefore the hardest worker in the family.

F.7

Some husbands refuse to help with household responsibilities, leaving the women with multiple duties, both in the labour force and at home.[1] (F.7)

---

[1] This factor has been cited by some men as a reason for not hiring women – they are too weak and have too much housework. Some enterprises give entrance tests to candidates of both sexes, but automatically eliminate the females. Others admit that they would rather employ a C level male than an A level female. (Jul. 8)

Rural women are more burdened than their urban counterparts. They are expected to work on even terms in the fields with men, to take produce to markets on poles in less developed communes – and still do housework. At times, as in the case of the Dai women, they weave and spin as well. (Jul. 7)

F.8

Mom! An ant!

妈妈！妈……妈蚁！

高世诔

Women are weak. (F.8)

A famous Mongolian, Ulan, who inspired an opera based on her life, spoke out in 1983 against discriminatory practices, saying, "I don't think women have the same chances (today) as we did when we joined the Revolution in the 1930s and 40s. I led a whole troop of men and no one disobeyed, even though I am a woman."[1] (Jul. 6)

Some of the problems of women were summarized at the Fifth National Women's Congress in September 1983. These included:

— "discrimination in job assignment and promotion;
— recurrence of female infanticide;
— preference for boy babies;
— sales of brides and other abuses of women;
— the persistence of feudal ideas;
— the influence of bourgeois ideas from abroad;
— slackness in punishing law violators."
(Sept. 3)

---

[1] Women are not satisfied with their progress in the hierarchy of the labour force and the Party. A few women hold important posts. In 1983, for example, a woman was elected chairman of the Sixth National Committee of the Chinese People's Political Consultative Conference. (June 18) But these women are usually appointed at an older age while the government's policy is to promote younger men. Representatives of women's groups are demanding that "younger women administrative staff members should enjoy the same opportunities for promotion as men." (June 28)

Lei Jiequiong, the 78-year old chairman of the Law Committee of the National People's Congress and of the All-

China Federation, as well as the China Association for Promoting Democracy, pointed out in 1983 that "sex discrimination and female infanticide are only visible manifestations of the invisible patriarchal partiality that persists despite all the rules and laws written since liberation on political and economic equality." (Aug. 23)

In the first six months of 1983, 26 women aged 31 to 52 years were elected leaders in 24 districts, counties or administrations in Tianjing, illustrating that changes are taking place in the status of women. However women are seeking more than token appointments. They are asking for maximum visibility at the national level to serve as an example.

Women with strong personalities or positions of influence are often blamed for dishonest motives and actions of leading cadres.[1]

F.9   *Modern wifely support*

新编《王宝钏》   王允沆

Feminine diplomacy

"夫人外交"   刘克勤

Eight "ordinary women" from leading cadres' families "signed a proposal that wives should not interfere with their husband's work .... Wives not interfering in their husbands' work and queens not eager to hear about state affairs," they recalled, "were praised as virtues in ancient China." (Nov. 5, June 4) (F.9)

---

[1]   Wives are accused, for example, of trying to prevent their husbands from retiring; of helping sons through legal or illegal means to evade the front-line service in the armed forces; and of taking plane rides to choose sons-in-law. Some women object to the blame placed on women for the misdeeds of men. "It is unfair to shunt all responsibility to women," they state. "That is what feudal writers of historical stories used to do. They found a woman to blame for the downfall of every dynasty." (Jul. 12)

The modern lifestyle and aspirations of women in China today are reflected in the fact that city girls now attend beauty clinics which have sprung up within the past three years. At these clinics, some women resort to cosmetic surgery to modify their facial features. Girls at the Health Beauty School in Beijing, established in 1981, explained their presence there to gain or lose weight, but mainly to gain beauty and to develop self-confidence.[1]

Young women at times face difficult decisions when they wish to combine conventional feminine interests with professional development. At the Chemical Engineering Department of one university, for example, some of the female students had fiancés who did not wish them to continue their studies because, as husbands, these young men did not look forward to sharing the housework. In brief the reaction of the female students was: " . . . it seems that if a woman is to have a career, she can only go to the extreme, that is, to completely forfeit the peace and quiet of normal family life . . . . If we choose an easier life and give up our careers, we will feel guilty for not living up to the expectations of our people and our country. The pursuit of a career will leave us little time for a personal life, but on the other hand, we will derive from our careers a higher sense of happiness."[2]

Male heads of families are "bowing" to the lifestyles of young independent women today, realizing that they cannot persist in the "autocratic" traditions of the past without leading to the break-up of the family unit. Working daughters who reside at home, for example, still contribute to the family income, but deduct the two yuan necessary for a permanent wave to avoid confrontation with a reluctant father.[3]

An active women's liberation movement is convinced that if women have "self-respect and the determination to improve themselves and to win over the whole society," they will eventually achieve "real sexual equality."[4]

F.10

Beautiful – or not

葵不葵   王炬

Making oneself "beautiful" while destroying the flowers. (F.10)

---

[1] "I don't want to be just a complacent and devoted mother as Chinese women are usually required to be," explained one of the girls at the school. "I want to find what I am really like – so that I can be more energetic and self-assured." (Aug. 7)

[2] **Women of China**, Feb. 1984, p. 16.

[3] **China Reconstructs**, July 1982.

[4] **Women of China**, Feb. 1984, p. 16.

Improved economic conditions have led to changes in the lifestyle of children as well as adults. The aim is that all the country's 300 million children gradually receive better and more varied clothing, toys, books, and cultural facilities.

Changes in the cultural environment of children contrast with pre-1978 conditions. (F.12, F.13)

F.12

Then: Only roadside puppet shows for our children

以前，为儿童演出的，只有街头「变把和」耍猴儿」（扁担木偶戏）

Children of urban cadres are surrounded by material affluence. (F.11)

F.11

Dad working.

Mother learning

童　话　*Me, doll – sitting*　蔡振华

爸爸在工作　　妈妈在学习　　我在看宝宝

F.13

Now: Children's own shows, theatre

儿童剧场

如今，不仅有儿童剧院、剧团，还有专为儿童开设的影院和剧场

90

F.14

(Curtain call by certain children's merchandise)

谢　　幕　　　　　　　　孙以增

——亲爱的小朋友，"六一"节已过，明年再见！

*Dear friends, see you next year
on Children's Day*

Both at the parental and official
levels there is a call for increasing
output for children: material (F.14),
cultural (F.15).

F.15

——小朋友，作家叔叔还没有把剧本写好，
再等一会儿，好不好？　　　　　韦启美

*Sorry! The playwright is still working
on the play. Please bear with me another
few minutes.*

"There are not many good children's books in China in recent years because too much emphasis has been put on long articles for adults."[1]

F.16

Repetitious contents of children's books. (F.16)

包围圈　　*Children's readers*　　乐小英

In an effort to increase the variety of books, the Children's Publishing House[2] issues an increasing number of translations of foreign books, i.e., from Yugoslavia, Romania, Japan, Canadam and other countries. The Secretary General of the Chinese Writers' Association welcomes these translations since "a good book", as he stated, "may surpass the boundaries of nations, and belong to the children all over the world . . . . Many contemporary writers make it their duty to help children, especially pre-schoolers, know the world, and encourage them to develop their imagination." (Jul. 1)

---

[1]　Statement by a translator at People's Literature Publishing House during a panel discussion on children's literature. **Women of China,** June 1984, p. 38.

[2]　Established in 1955, the Children's Publishing House was closed from 1966 to 1976 during the Cultural Revolution, but it has published a total of 205 million books with 1,150 titles. (Jul. 1)

With a population of close to 1 billion, China has intensified its birth control programme so as to reduce the strain on its resources for personal consumption and to allow for an accelerated rate of capital accumulation.

F.17

Standard of living

National economy

Unplanned

计划外生育

Since 1978 there has been an unrelenting campaign to promote and uphold the one-child family.[1] (F.17)

多 余 的 负 担 *Surplus burden* 金三（沈阳）

---

[1] The general approach to the birth control programme is a combination of publicity, persuasion, and easy accessibility to contraception. However there are variations at provincial and local levels. Comparisons in standard of living among units are used to show the effectiveness of the various programmes. Rongcheng County in Shandong Province, for example, had the honour in 1982 of having one of the lowest birth rates in the country – 10.02 per 1000 compared to a national rate of 14.55 (June 14)

In one commune (Quijia), the need for better birth control programmes was shown in economic terms as follows: 1981 grain output was 160 per cent more than 1949, but per capita output showed only a 70 per cent increase due to the population increase and land lost to new housing. (June 14)

Sichuan Province, with one tenth of the country's population, spends about 30 million yuan each year on its population control programme. The effect of its population increase is that while its total industrial and agricultural output is fifth among 29 provinces, autonomous regions and municipalities, Sichuan ranks 25th in per capita output. With 12,000 family planning workers in its factories, mines and villages working in cooperation with local doctors, the birth rate has been reduced from 4 per cent in 1970 to 1.5 per cent in 1982. Still, the province is far from satisfied and "plans to stay in the lead of the country's family planning drive." (June 17)

For China as a whole, the present population growth rate is 1.4 per cent. Government policy is that "it must be reduced to 0.95 in the next 20 years (through family planning) to keep the country's population within 1.2 billion at the end of the century." (June 17)

The one-child family requirement is generally relaxed for rural families and returned overseas Chinese.[1]

Traditional norms make it easier for families to accept the one-child concept when the first-born is a boy. (F.18)

Women's groups in China as well as the government are actively encouraging the equal acceptance of first-born girls.[2]

---

[1] A variety of penalties are imposed for having more than one child, such as punitive charges for schooling and other services paid from collective funds.

Some cadres, in order to produce the impression that family planning is working in their area, refuse to report all births, thereby depriving the newborn of legal status as well as grain rations. (**China Reconstructs**, July 1982, p. 37)

[2] For example, in Nov.-Dec. 1983, the Jiangxi Provincial Women's Federation joined with the "Provincial Party committee, government, trade union, Communist Youth League, and departments of judiciary, education, public health and publicity − 17 units in all" on a month-long campaign to "sensitize the public to the legal provisions that will strengthen their hands in combatting feudal and bourgeois thinking and in cracking down on crimes against women and children." During the campaign, one commune member admitted that she "was so eager to have a boy to keep the family line that she gave away her first-born daughter. 'I was unaware that it was a crime to desert an infant girl,' she told other women in her village." "Female infanticide and the mistreatment of mothers of baby girls" are " remnants of feudal thinking" which the All-China Federation of Women includes in its programmes to protect the legitimate interests of women. (**Women of China**, April 1984, p. 12)

F.18

并非 "三句半"   王景峰

Punch line

Incentives are offered to parents who accept the one-child concept.[1] The children have priority access to educational and all other state facilities and are guaranteed jobs in the future. They present a new and exciting challenge to their teachers who describe them as "spoiled, self-centred, wayward, domineering and temperamental." When they enter kindergarten for the first time, they "obey no one and cry easily." (Jul. 15)

The faculties of these children are generally well developed due to the concentrated attention they receive. Parents are expected to respond to them without becoming "irritated" and should not "hit the child."[2] (F.19)

Hundred thousand and one Why's

F.19 十万零一个为什么   赵学禹

爸，天为什么是蓝色的？
Dad, why is the sky blue?

…影子为什么跟我走？
Why do shadows follow me?

…鸟为什么掉不下来？
Why do birds not fall down?

为什么……？
Why …

爸，您为什么打我？
Why do you hit me?

---

[1] In 1980 it was estimated that fringe benefits to cooperating parents in Beijing amounted to approximately 20 per cent of an employee's income. (**Beijing Review**, July 28, 1980, p. 6)

[2] A mother who displayed impatience in a restaurant when her child broke two spoons in succession evoked "murmurs among others in the restaurant about her outburst," and was scolded by the waitress who declared "that hitting did no good, for the girl was too small to know the spoons could break." (**Women of China**, Feb. 1984, p. 40)

F.20

Parents dote on their single child
in whom all their aspirations are
concentrated. (F.20, F.21)

F.21

F.22

Which do you want?

Just plain bun

宝贝，想吃什么？

窝头！

和

非

Doting parents.[1] (F.22, F.23)

F.23

Restaurant scene

餐厅一角

---

[1] An increasing lack of community spirit has been found among one-family children and this has been linked to the "doting" parents. A child had a fight at school, for example, and his father turned up the next day. Without any discussion with the teacher the father shouted at the pupils: "Who beat my child? Don't dare any of you touch him again. I'll teach you a lesson." In another case, a child reported to his parents that he was praised for tightening the shoe-laces of another. The father in this situation angrily reacted that the child was sent to school to learn, not to serve others. (Jul. 15)

The attitudes contrast with the early 1970s and before when "concern for others" and "to serve others" were popular mottos.

Special programmes have been set up to help only children develop a collective spirit. Children's summer camps are becoming increasingly popular,[1] but the best camps such as the children's club at the Temple of Heaven, Beijing, are reserved for only children. (Jul. 16) Parents at times resort to underhand methods to get their children accepted into these key camps and other key institutions.[2]

F.24   *Children's Paintings – Display*

当 场 露 馅   *Caught red-handed*   韩冬 孙泽良

Parental guidance. (F.24, F.25)

F.25

The story is told of a child who "could draw an eagle swooping down on a chicken. But he could draw nothing else. In fact, the original picture was drawn by his father who told him to copy it again and again. He was not allowed to draw anything else." (Nov. 19)

神乎其神   *Whiz kid*   张乐平

---

[1] In summer 1983, for example, activities were planned by 25 national scientific societies, children's centres, neighbourhood committees and the press. The China Institute of Communications had the largest camp (15,000 children) with activities that included lectures, films, studies on telegraphy, as well as visits to satellite ground stations and communication facilities. In eathquake-sensitive areas, camps by the Seismological Society included seismological activities. Others focused on ecology, forestry, space navigation, insects, meteorology, and ship-building. Urban neighbourhood committees organized games, reviewed lessons and offered films and art programmes. (Jul. 9)

[2] Key camps and educational institutions are prestigious ones, graduation from which ensures entry into others up the scale, and ultimately, to the best jobs.

F.26

都有一本难念的经

王 健

The one child in a family is subjected to severe parental pressure to
achieve at the academic level.[1]
(F.26, F.27)

F.27

Baby failed in phys ed at school

儿 子 体 育 不 及 格

The demands imposed by parents are condemned in the Chinese press which publishes letters from children complaining about the harsh treatment by parents disappointed at their school marks.[2]

---

[1] The Chinese Children's Publishing House expressed surprise that translations of Hans Christian Andersen's **The Ugly Duckling** and Oscar Wilde's **The Happy Prince**, issued in its Literature Treasure-House For Pre-School Children series, were best-sellers since, "many parents are over-anxious to feed their children more arithmetic and phsyics, hoping they will get into key primary schools." (Jul. 1)

[2] A teacher, for example, "discovered that one of her students . . . was in low spirits and would not talk" after an arithmetic test. "She learned from another student who lived nearby . . . that his (the first student's) father often beat and yelled at him for his poor results at school." This time the student had only 42 marks on his test and "was sure that his father would beat him again. Therefore he lied to his father that the teacher had not let him know the marks." This case was resolved in a cooperative programme set up between father, teacher and child, but it is indicative of the academic environment within which the children operate. (**Women of China**, June 1984, p. 2)

Academic demands on the child are overwhelming. (F.28, F.29)

F.28

爱 乎 *Homework overload* 青岛 张 纲

Even Ne Zha, a mythical super youth with three heads, six arms, and two wheels for feet, finds it difficult to cope. (F.30)

F.29

Test tomorrow! 明天要测验

F.30

哪吒败阵 *Overwhelmed* 范其恢

F.31

In general, society imposes demanding standards on children. (F.31, F.32)

However excessive these demands may be, the children enjoy more freedom today than they did in pre-1978 China. The Chinese now describe that period as one of over-control and regimentation. A popular saying is that the toilet was the children's "free market" up to 1976. That was the only place where they were free to talk and laugh at school. (Jul. 15)

At kindergarten they were required to line up to drink water, to wash their hands, and everyone had to start eating at the same time. Now, unquestioned conformity is no longer required. Children have time off for games of their choice and can play indoors or outdoors as they wish during recreation periods. The aim is to develop more perceptive, mature and independent-thinking adults in the future. At the same time, steps are being taken to ensure that emerging egotism under the one-child family system does not counter-balance this goal.

F.32

Some producers demand adult performance from children

In contrast to the era of the Cultural Revolution when the political consciousness of youth in China took the form of the Red Guard Movement, today's youth reflects the influences of increasing wealth and reoriented aspirations. Young people operate in a relaxed social environment. **Chinese Youth News** supports this environment: "We should protect, support and guide young people to work hard to create a better life, and should not concentrate on the width of trousers, the height of heels and on hair styles." The paper goes on to stress that China should not return to the "socialist poverty" advocated between 1966 and 1976 by those who "undermined the name of socialism . . . when the populace was a monotonous sea of blue and grey." (Nov. 18)

There is some concern as to how freedom of choice is exercised by the youth today.[1] (F.33)

F.33

---

[1] There are now, for example, only a few members in the Communist Youth League and meetings are infrequent and superficial. In most rural areas, the League no longer functions. (June 10) Some university departments have difficulty attracting students to join the Party. (July 11)

On the other hand, there are youth who reflect the moral, intellectual and physical development at which government aims. (Nov. 30) These young people become involved in the "Serve the People" volunteer teams promoted across the country in recent years. In December 1982, 1,269 such teams in Hangzhou Province helped 521 childless, elderly couples, including the sick and disabled. (Dec. 12) Similar projects include Social Practice Week held in December 1983, co-sponsored by the Central Committee of the Communist Youth League and the All-China Students Federation "to widen the students' horizons and strengthen ties with working people." (Dec. 12)

The average youth in China today is concerned with personal advancement.[1] Most see education as the means to realize their aspirations, and as a result, there is an overwhelming enthusiasm for education in the country.

> The quest for education is not fazed by inadequate facilities. (F.34)

Up to the end of the Cultural Revolution, access to institutions of higher learning was dependent on one's political qualifications rather than academic capabilities. As a result of the admission criteria, educational standards were compromised. In 1978, academic-based entrance examinations were reinstituted. Millions of students all over the country now compete in these examinations.

F.34

无
题

张
久

University student hall

There has been an uncontrolled surge in commercialized test aids to help students prepare for entrance examinations. (F.35)

F.35

Which way?

迷 阵   陈惠龄

Variety of entrance test aids for students

---

[1] Expression of this concern today, as opposed to pre-1978, is largely influenced by increasing material comforts and exposure to images of affluence abroad through radio and television, and by an influx of foreigners and returned overseas Chinese.

The Responsibility Movement permits some flexibility of movement among rural youth who have been basically locked into their existing work environment for life. However, the key to legitimate mobility is higher education.

F.36

Many rural youth strive to enter institutions of higher learning to achieve the freedom of mobility. (F.36)

飞　了　　　*Fly away*　　　陈景凯

F.37

闹　学　　*Obstructions to schooling*　　陈景和

In the past, and in some backward regions today, farmers de-emphasize education to the disadvantage of the rural youth.[1] (F.37)

---

[1] As a result of the Responsibility Movement, farmers are more affluent and can afford to contribute to the education of their children, while mechanization reduces the demand for the number of farm hands. As representative of the modern farmer, Ma Fuxi "had a problem: should his 13-year-old boy stay at school or help him with his duck-raising business?" Ma decided on education since he realized that duck-raising, prosperous as it was now, would be further advanced in the future with "scientific and cultural knowledge." (Nov. 17)

Heilongjiang Province has now stipulated that "any young person who has not received middle school education has no right to be a farmer and will not be allowed to settle in the village." (Nov. 17)

Rural youth and others from disadvantaged backgrounds, such as national minorities with different languages and customs, are given compensatory entry points to institutions of higher learning to allow for shortcomings in their preparatory training.

Some who benefited from compensatory admission points encounter problems of adjustment.[1] (F.38, F.39)

F.39

Write the 26 letters of the English alphabet

"My test paper"

The new economic and social order in China enables the youth to progress more in relation to their capabilities than their political orientation as in the past. There is scope for relaxation and more occupational and locational mobility. However, new problems have emerged.

Foremost among these are unemployment and the need to be aggressively competitive for economic survival. Displacement on the farm through mechanization: the phasing out of the Iron Rice Bowl which no longer ensures the retention of jobs in the family line; the focus on productivity which no longer guarantees a job after graduation, are all problems affecting youth. These are dealt with in different sections of this book. Cultural patterns which have been subjected to foreign influences also create new social pressures. The weakening of family ties as the result of the more material oriented society of today has left youth somewhat disoriented and has led to an increasing incidence of delinquency.

---

[1] A college freshman describes some incidents during the "first year of agony" such as: "A student from the countryside proudly tells his classmates he had read all the books in his county library. Later, he was at a loss when he saw the college library." Another situation mentioned was that many students memorize the key points in books which teachers summarize for them in school, but "in college (they) find it hard to grasp essential meanings by themselves. Some will busily attempt to take down every word the teacher says in class." (Dec. 15)

Still, many able and dynamic young people fanning out from large cities to the border regions, are grasping the opportunities which present themselves to contribute to a modern China.

The National People's Congress, meeting in June 1983, expressed confidence in the contributions that China's 250 million youth will make to the tasks set by the Congress of "stepping up economic construction and improving social conduct and the financial situation radically in the coming 5 years." "Chinese youth of today," stated the Secretary of the China Youth League at the Congress, "will carry out these tasks just as young people in the 1950s tackled the major construction projects. They will also go to work where conditions are hardest and act as a shock force in the new 'long march' towards building a powerful, modern, socialist country." (June 22)

F.40

Mother's mother   Paternal grandmother

姥姥来了

妈妈买菜

Mom's grocery basket

奶奶来了

Grandma is coming   王金海

F.41[1]

Mother-in-law

Mom

辰 1982

妈＜快曹一品锅

蔡振华

Strained relationships between wives and their mothers-in-law. (F.40, F.41)

The average woman in pre-1949 China was at the level of a second-class citizen. The status of young girls and unmarried women was even lower: they were third-class citizens and treated as assets which could be sold in times of need. Once married, a woman moved to the home of her in-laws to render service, and was entirely at the mercy of her mother-in-law who played an important role in the family.[2]

Changed social attitudes and economic circumstances have given the modern wife a feeling of independence vis-à-vis her mother-in-law. Many neighbourhood committees have established groups where mothers-in-law exchange ideas on how to get along with their daughters-in-law. The head of one such group in Beijing explained that "mother-in-law problems concern many street committee advisers because nowadays younger women are educated and independent . . . . They do not have traditional attitudes (of respect) towards their mothers-in-law." (Aug. 30)

---

[1] Fish soup for mother-in-law; roast pork, chicken for mother.

[2] During a publicity month in 1983 organized by Jiangxi Provincial Women's Federation to advise women about "protection of the legitimate rights of women and children," it was proven that in rural areas mothers-in-law still exercise control over some women. In a case cited, for example, a widow revealed that "her parents-in-law prevented her from remarrying for fear that she would take possession of the three rooms she had lived in with her husband." The organizers succeeded in upholding her rights under the Marriage Law provision that "husbands and wives have the right to inherit each other's property." Before the end of the campaign, "those who had . . . badly treated their daughters-in-law admitted their faults to the publicity office of the Women's Federation and some pledged not to do it again." (**Women of China**, April 1984, p. 13)

F.42

拉大锯，扯大锯　姥姥家坑上唱大戏　　　*Nanny's song*　　　郭国林

Mother-in-law helps with care of the children. (F.42)

The housing shortage in urban areas and the higher standard of living have given rise to the nuclear family as a norm. Mothers-in-law also increasingly prefer to be on their own rather than tied down to their children as baby-sitters. A joint-family system where in-laws have separate but adjoining residences sometimes occurs.[1] The mother-in-law in this case continues to play an important supporting role, especially in the up-bringing of the children.

---

[1] This pattern is replacing the open extended family in prosperous rural areas.

F.43

镜破重圆   *Broken mirror repaired*   熊国昭

Neighbourhood committees have been helpful in mediating family disputes.[1] (F.43)

The divorce rate, which averages 400,000 a year, is an indication of the independence of women in China today. A study of the causes for divorce in 1982 identified urban living as well as the fact that an increasing number of peasant women no longer tolerate bullying by their husbands. The record year for divorce was 1953 when women who had been forced into marriages prior to 1949 sought their freedom under the new laws established by the People's Republic. (Jul. 23)

A conservative element in China sees the high divorce rate as reflecting a tendency towards a bourgeois way of life. Lei Jieqiong, chairman of the All-China Women's Federation, however, explains that this is one means whereby women are moving towards emancipation from "feudal mental fetters." (Aug. 23)

[1]   **Women of China**, April 1984, p. 13.

The Deputy Director of the Civil Division of the Supreme People's Court identifies the main cause of broken marriages today as male chauvenism and the involvement of third parties. (Jul. 23)

Third party involvement is a growing problem reflecting affluence, mobility and new social standards. This is a situation which the older generation finds difficult to handle. A leader at a mothers-in-law group meeting of a Beijing neighbourhood committee saw "a third person entering the marriage relationship" as a new problem which both embarrasses mothers-in-law and baffles the committee leaders . . . . "We leaders haven't worked out a proper way to deal with the problem," she stated. (Aug. 30) The situation facing the neighbourhood committees is complicated by the fact that modern emancipated wives no longer accept the outside relationships of their husbands which in the past were part of the norm.

The social upheaval resulting from the high divorce rate will seem a less insurmountable problem in the years ahead when the emancipated wives of today retire to become conciliatory members of the neighbourhood committees of the future.

Women no longer passively accept male chauvenism. (F.44)

F.44

Not silent night

不平静的夜　　徐建民

G. SOCIAL IMPACT OF FOREIGN INFLUENCES

In order to accelerate its economic development after years of relative isolation, China has actively expanded its contacts with foreign countries since 1978. The result is an influx of foreigners to the country.[1]

G.1

哼．崇洋媚外   徐鹏飞

Reinforced by special privileges in China, most foreigners project a relatively affluent life-style which some local Chinese resent. On the other hand, others are glad to see China part of the international community. For some, the presence of foreigners is an opportunity to practise the foreign language they are studying. (G.1)

---

[1] These might be representatives of official or unofficial trade, political or cultural delegations; teachers of a wide range of subjects from language courses to business administration and technology; foreign experts working on Chinese-owned or joint projects; and a multitude of tourists providing foreign exchange.

Social Impact of Foreign Influences

Increasing numbers of radios and television sets combine with the presence of foreigners to bring about social and cultural changes. Cartoonists point critically to some of these changes in the following manner:

High heels on the farm. (G.2)

Advertisement for lotion to **prevent** tanning overlooks sun bathers on the beach. (G.3)

The refusal to wear a hard hat which would disturb her permanent wave leaves a worker unprotected against industrial accidents. (G.4)

G.2

足尖舞

庸 非

Tap dance

G.3

Unique way to protect your skin from the sun

海滨的幽默 *Beach advertising* 马瑞洁

G.4

烦恼皆因强出头

白水 明德

Asking for trouble

112

During the Great Leap Forward in 1955, fashion shows were encouraged in the cities to reinforce the idea of a movement towards a new and bright future for China. City dwellers and intellectuals flourished under the banner of "Let 100 flowers bloom" until 1957 when an imminent economic collapse was avoided by economic, but also social adjustments. A reversal of the life-style which encouraged high fashion set in and criticisms were launched against "over-indulgence". With today's new affluence, high fashions are again in vogue.

G.5

Fashion show, Peiking. (Self excluded)

《叶浅予画展》最近在中国美术馆开幕，展出的作品中有一部分是漫画。叶浅予同志的创作活动已经有五十五年，他早期的作品主要是漫画，这次展出的漫画有《王先生别传》、《小陈留京外史》、《我的童年》、《战时重庆》、《天堂记》等作品和其他单幅漫画。[1]

Committee members

Designer

Seamstress

Interpreter

1982 reproduction of 1955 cartoon of Beijing Fashion show, by Yeh Chien-Yu. (G.5)

[1] Translation: "The recent exhibit of veteran artist Yeh Chien-Yu's work was held at China's Arts Pavilion . . . . Comrade Yeh's artistic activities have spanned 55 years." . . . In 1955 the new fashions were not intended for everyone. Note the contrasts in the "designer" styles and the "old" styles of the designer herself, her committee members and employees.

G.6

Example of modern fashion trend.[1]
(G.6)

Shows-off U.S. T-shirt in cold weather

There is much discussion in China on the relative merits and drawbacks of western-style clothes.[2] Those favouring the new fashions point out that the "Mao jacket" now accepted as a norm was not a Chinese creation but was imported from the West as a uniform after the 1911 Revolution. (June 10)

---

[1] The demand for T-shirts reached such proportions that fraudulent distribution practices resulted in a shortage in state-owned shops in spite of a 40 per cent increase in output that reached 9.5 million in the first 5 months of 1983. (Jul. 6)

[2] The shift to western styles is widespread. "This summer (1983) has seen the arrival of a gallery of new styles for women: nylon dresses, silk dresses with elegant decorations, shirts in different cuts, and close-fitting dresses with high necks and slit skirts, popular in China before the Cultural Revolution . . . . Even boys are putting on dotted shirts, though they occasionally meet with disapproving eyes from elders who regard them as too westernized." (June 16)

The "uniform designs and dull colours" are being replaced by "fancy dress (which) has been coming out of the closets." (Oct. 11)

Jeans and bell-bottom trousers are often associated with questionable fringe elements in society. (G.7)

G.7

Film: The Guardian of the Horses[1]

牧马人
－电影简介－

一那姓许的真是傻帽儿！

"We disagree"

For some designers, "there is no reason why young people cannot wear jeans and coloured shirts," "but clothing that exposes the bosom, back and shoulders is not suited to Chinese customs." Jeans and bell-bottom trousers are regarded as exotic, but defended as expressing "young people's daring to probe and practise in life." (Oct. 11)

---

[1] The film, **Guardian of the Horses,** which the couple are commenting on is the story of a young man, Chu, who was sent from the city to the steppes to work as a herdsman after being accused of rightist tendencies during the Cultural Revolution. Chu was rehabilitated after the overthrow of the Gang of Four, and became a school teacher.

Chu's father had immigrated to the United States 30 years before without waiting for the birth of his son. He had returned on a visit to China and tried without success to induce Chu to come to the U.S. with him. "I love my country and my people who have stood by me in my difficulties," Chu said. The youth in the cartoon disagree. "This Chu is an idiot," they declare. "He should leave China."

Literary works also reflect foreign influences.[1]

Publishing house produces only 3 types of books: love stories, westerns, and detective novels. (G.8)

G.8

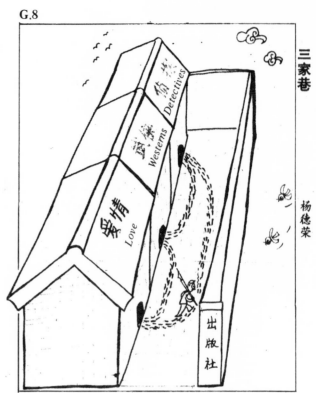

Three Family Lane (Lane is publisher)

G.9

(Robbers: Western and Kong-Fu fictions)
路　　劫 *Highway robbery* 徐学廉

The usurpation of Chinese literature by foreign themes. (G.9)

---

[1] Foreign literature is welcomed in China, but there is concern as to its excessive commercialization and the content of the material being popularized. The Director of the Commercial Press, for example, has increased the number of translations of important foreign thinkers, such as Aristotle, Locke, Hegel and Paul Samuelson, the Americain economist, in order to place this literature at the disposal of the public. "Once a nation indulges in smug complacency," explains the Director, "it loses the nutrients from the infusion of foreign cultures, and its own culture dries up and becomes ossified." (Je. 21)

G.10

G.11 *Film credits*[1]

Deputy
producer

Assistant
cameraman

Assistant
stagehand

Stage
adviser

Film
editor

Assistant . . .

Sponsor . . .

短片不短 *No short films anymore* 丁原平

Modifications in behaviour due to
foreign influences. (G.10, G.11,
G.12)

G.12 *Rise and fall of hair style*

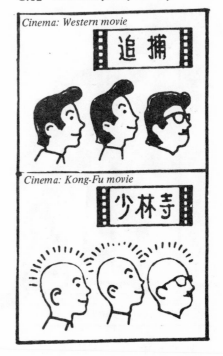

---

[1] Lengthy names of producers, advisers, assistants, sponsors, etc. In the past such detailed film credits were not given. This
is intended to ridicule exaggerated imitation.

Films from Romania, France, England, the U.S.A., Japan and other countries can be seen in Beijing almost any day. (G.13)

At times "tricks of foreign film-makers are copied mechanically to the point where fist-fighting of an exotic style and unhealthy tendencies are luridly pictured to regale Chinese audiences.[1]

Youth are seen as most susceptible to the influences of foreign media. A researcher at the Chinese Youth Academy of Social Sciences explained that "some young people are really naive. They see a few movies or read a few stories about the influence of the West, and decide it is Paradise." At the same time it was pointed out that those receptive to the "lure of the West" are "only a minority." "Look at the thousands of study groups across the country! . . . They are not wasting their time (and they represent) our country's future," the Academy stated. (June 10)

Imitation. (G.14)

G.13

— *Stage show* —

Kong-Fu films beat educational and children's films

擂台上（原载《电影评介》）　　许小铭

There is no intent to stop the influx of foreign films, rather to closely monitor their content. At a joint conference of the Chinese Ministries of Culture and of Radio and Television in November 1983, a statement was issued to the effect that "Chinese youth should be given access to foreign films portraying patriotism and opposing feudalism, and those adapted from world-famous works including biographies of historical figures, as long as the content is healthy." (Nov. 30)

The social, economic and even political impact of foreign films will increase as cinemas and television become more widespread with the provision of electricity to remote areas. Other factors contributing to an increasing foreign impact include the large number of translations of foreign works; accessibility to foreign editions by the many who are now attracted to foreign languages[2]; an ever-increasing number of foreigners in all parts of the country; more and more Chinese delegations travelling abroad; government-sponsored, as well as private, Chinese scholars and students returning from studies abroad. The growing effect of foreign influences is monitored by the government and counter-campaigns will be launched at any stage where the impact is considered undesirable.

G.14

Modernized

Old classic performance

---

[1] **Beijing Review**, July 14, 1980.

[2] Japanese, English and French are widely studied by educated youth as a pastime.

H. CULTURAL CONTAMINATION

H.1

Distortion of history and reality by fabricating fancy stories. (H.1)

Twisted image

失真（原载《河南日报》） 凤 岐

(Reality vs literary works)

There is "unprecedented prosperity in literature and art" and "remarkable works" have appeared since the Cultural Revolution period in China.[1] Deng Xiaoping heralded this change by affirming that "any artistic creation that provided education, enlightenment, entertainment and aesthetic enjoyment on a scale, grand or small, written in a serious or humorous vein, lyrical or philosophical, should have a place in the garden of literature and art." (Nov. 23)

Resurgence of the arts has been accompanied by unacceptable practices against which the government has launched a "Cultural Contamination" campaign.

Among the practices attacked by the campaign are:
- "polluting people's minds with unhealthy mentality, works and performances;
- indifference that art should serve the people and socialism;
- lack of enthusiasm in depicting and praising the revolutionary history and heroic deeds of the Party and the people;
- depicting gloomy aspects of society, even distorting history and reality by fabricating fancy stories;
- spreading pornography and religion."
(Nov. 4)

---

[1] After the establishment of the People's Republic in 1949, all forms of art were subordinated to the state. Cultural activities were confined to the production of slogans, paintings of peasant and working-class life, economic and political-cultural beautification, and the creation of revolutionary songs and films. With the Cultural Revolution came a climax to the era of cultural restraint, and there was a literary outburst following its collapse.

Writers, artists, actors, and film makers who were previously silenced have now returned to develop traditional as well as experimental modern themes. For example, a 67-year-old painter, who suffered under the Cultural Revolution, is working on a three-year project extending scenes painted by a master painter of the Northern Song Dynasty (960–1127) to reveal the "magnificent buildings, streets and daily lives of outer and inner cities and imperial palaces which existed under the dynasty." (Je. 18) Zhu Muzhi, Chinese Minister of Culture in 1983, explained the change thus: "Taking communist ideology as the core did not mean filling a work of art with slogans or dogmas devoid of reality." (Nov. 23)

Following the collapse of the Cultural Revolution, people read anything they could find.[1] To capture the market, writers hurriedly turned out a multiplicity of works, many of which were of poor quality.

H.2

Literary work — impressive but no content. (H.2)

H.3

如此创作　*Creative writer*　杨成忠

Some writers' "creativity" was limited to how thoroughly they could re-work the same theme. (H.3)

Exploiting the surge in demand for books. (H.4)

H.4

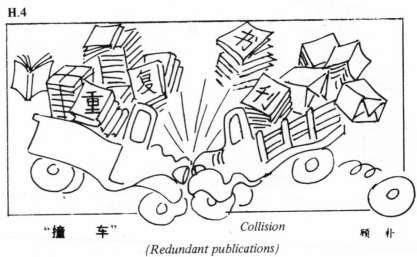

"撞车"　*Collision*　顾朴
(Redundant publications)

121

H.5

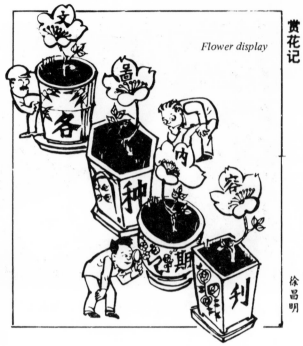

Flower display

赏花记

徐昌明

Pots: Different publications
Contents: Same flowers

Recycled works to maximize market exposure. (H.5, H.6)

H.6

新瓶装旧酒

New bottle, old wine

The public has joined the outcry against abuse by writers. A bookstore, for example, carried three collections by the same author from three different publishing houses. Asked if all three versions had the same stories, the clerk explained: "Some were the same, some different." The client, confused and feeling abused, wrote a letter of complaint to the newspaper. (Nov. 19)

H.7

天下文章一大抄　　　王健

读一些期刊有感

A copies from B; B from C; C from A, etc.

Respectful copying of the masters — whether as writers or painters — is part of the Chinese tradition,[1] but in some instances this practice has been reduced to one of plagiarism for selfish exploitation. (H.7, H.8, H.9)

H.8

文　丑 *Writer as clown* 刘庆涛

(Stealing fruits from others)

H.9

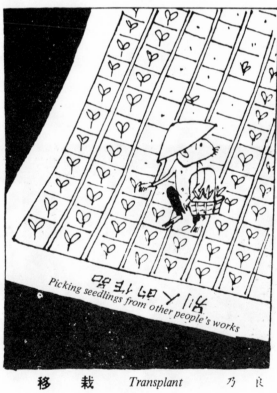

移　栽　*Transplant*　乃良

---

[1] With regard to painting for example, "the sense of the supreme value of the tradition laid upon the individual artist the duty to devote at least part of his time and energy to copying the works of old masters." (Michael Sullivan. The heritage of Chinese art, in **The Legacy of China**, Raymond Dawson ed., London, Oxford University Press, 1964, p. 208.)

An article in **China Daily** refers to a young worker who copied one dozen novels, signed his name and published a collection of "his works". When apprehended, he explained that he saw this as a means to be promoted a "white collar cadre". (Aug. 27)

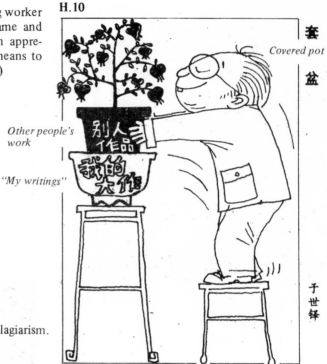

H.10

Covered pot

Other people's work

"My writings"

Additional conceptions of plagiarism.
(H.10, H.11, H.12)

H.11

文坛窃贼   *Literary theft*

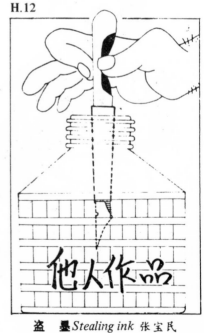

H.12

盗 墨 *Stealing ink*

H.13

"Great works" = casserole of extracts from writings of others. (H.13)

H.14

Each word bears fruits of "hard work"

Questionable professional standards are now seen among journalists as well as others. (H.14)

H.15

*How to prepare an article with minimum
time and effort*

Formula writing:
Head — A. Title
        B. Quotation
        C. Quotation
Feet — E. . . .
        F. . . .
        G. . . .
In between (the filler) —
        Relate one's point of view
        Copy points of view from
          books
        If opinions asked, get ideas
          from the classics
Use paste-up throughout
Take a half a day to give summary
  report to audience. (H.15)

"The unilateral pursuit of 'making literature and art serve politics' did narrow one's approach and should be corrected, but the portrayal of 'secrets deep in one's heart', personal (trivialities) and the chewing out of one's own frustrations or sufferings would not broaden the approaches of socialist literature and art." (Nov. 14) Such works are therefore subjected to criticism.[1]

H.16 *Let's drink from the same spring*

Love themes offer commercial rewards, but are considered especially "poisoning" to the minds of the youth. (H.16)

---

[1] Concern is especially focused on the impact these works might have on the youth. This concern is not new. The author, Lu Xun, in **Letter from Peking** (1925), wrote: "My life belongs to me, and I can go forward in great strides on a road of my own choosing . . . . But when talking to young people, I'm faced with difficulties. Suppose I'm a blind man riding a blind horse and lead them to a path of danger, then I would be guilty of murdering many lives." (Nov. 26)

A writer in **China Daily** noted that whereas writers and artists should "listen to the voice of the peo-ple," some established writers consider their works above criticism. Others "are praised though they have serious defects." Such writers protect their works "like silly mothers who spoil their children" instead of correcting them.

Irresponsible critics:
— discouraging talent[1] (H.17)
— overpraise (H.18)

H.17

Poor daughter-in-law

难为媳妇　　　　　　江有生

公公：为什么不红烧？
婆婆：为什么不炖鸡汤？
小姑：为什么不炒鸡丁？

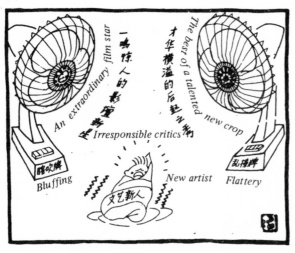

H.18

吹　不　得　　　孙光钊

Please don't blow too hard!

---

[1] Inlaws = critics; chicken = literary output; daughter-in-law = new talented writer. The discouragement suffered from irresponsible critics is similar to that experienced by a wife seeking recognition from new in-laws.

Some artists, like writers, have also compromised creativity, subordinating it to financial gains.

H.19

Recycled design.[1]
(H.19)

The magic wand

H.20

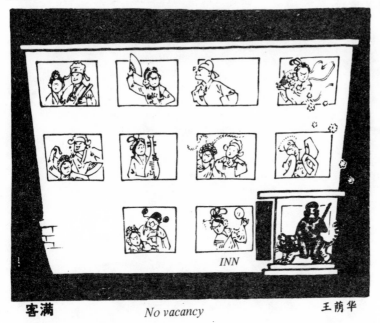

Frozen design.[2] (H.20)

No vacancy

---

[1] "My creations" represent a re-worked, market-tested design. This guarantees money like a magic wand.

[2] These are the 10-stamp designs used by a certain publishing house X in the illustrated section of a New Year's magazine. The designs sell well and no changes are allowed. The "No vacancy" sign indicates that all 10 spots are filled. The tiger controlled by an iron rod at the entrance ensures that no new design will try to enter.

H.21

机器画画 八年十用 地北偶诗 华君武画

无需生活，　　制不妨粗，
不用灵感，　　造不怕滥，
大笔一挥，　　快速操作，
曲曲弯弯。　　批量生产。
要水有水，　　敞开供应，
要山有山，　　多多益善。
立轴画竹，　　名利双收，
横幅画兰。　　驰骋画坛。
千张一律，　　恼煞唐寅，
有如翻版。　　气死罗丹。

The Robot Painter[1] (H 21)

No need for social life
      no need for inspiration.
He passes his brush zig zag:
        need water! it's there;
        need mountains! it's there.
With vertical strokes he creates bamboos;
      with horizontal ones, orchids.
One thousand sheets of paper – same images
      like reproductions.
One can produce in large numbers
      create any design,
      manipulate rapidly,
      produce large quantities,
      produce more and more
and achieve celebrity and fortune,
and gallop through artistic circles.

Much annoyed would be M. Tang Yin[2]
      and enraged to death Rodin.[3]

---

[1] Adapted from Li Shengheng's translation of the Chinese.

[2] Chinese painter, 1470–1523.

[3] French sculptor and painter, 1840–1917.

Artists who lack training and recognition but present themselves as experts. (H.22)

H.22

不用深入生活，也不要
文化修养，装了两节电池就
是艺术家。

No need to go to the streets
No need to have training
Put two batteries together
Voilà, an artist

Self-styled artists who seek to avoid established routine procedures. (H.24)

H.24

凡是鸭子难道就都应该
有本事下水吗？

Does every duck have
to swim in water?

Artists who bask in unwarranted recognition. (H.23)

H.23

我就喜欢人家吹吹。

I love blowing in the wind

Artists who break away from accepted standards and fall to the lowest levels. (H.25)

H.25

我自由了！

————*Free at last!*

玩具篇　　朱新建

H.26

"Slipshod" work.[1] (H.26)

"啦 啦" 队 (对某些歌曲的看法) *My opinion of certain songs* 李满仓

The "cultural pollution" campaign will be considered successful to the extent that "writers, artists and people working in the ideological field (who are) engineers of the human soul" enjoy the freedom of experimentation while adhering to "the four basic principles of:
   — the socialist road;
   — the Party's leadership;
   — people's democratic dictatorship; and
   — Marxism-Leninism—Mao Zedung Thought."
   (Nov. 4)

At the same time, the government points out clearly that serving the Revolution does not exclude constructive criticism. Writer Wang Meng, for example, was silenced in 1957 on the grounds that he was "destructive, anti-Party and anti-socialist," but he is now acclaimed for his willingness to point out "abuse" of power, stupidity in officialdom, human folly and moral corruption." (Jul. 7) The series of cartoons in this book also attest to the freedom accorded those engaged in the arts to register their concerns on varied aspects of society.

---

[1] The song here is a series of "La-la-la . . ." typifying mediocrity. An example of "bad taste" was seen at a performance arranged by the Chinese Musicians' Association at Tianjin in 1982 to commemorate the 41st Anniversary of Mao Zedung's speech at Yanan, 1942, dealing with the Chinese Communist Party's policies on literature and the arts. The lead singers's behaviour, "trying to follow the gestures of some foreign singers," reflected "loose behaviour . . . with the unhealthy tendency of looking forward to the money to be raised by the show." The audience was left "sickened and cheated" by the behaviour. "The show," summarized **China Daily**, "went under the flag of the Speech, but in reality it catered only to unhealthy tastes and has polluted the theatre." (Jul. 14)

PART II
THE MODERNIZATION PROCESS:
PROBLEMS

China launched a modernization drive in 1978 which has been accompanied by social, economic and political changes, as well as a rising standard of living. Although none of these changes has negated the political ideology of the country, they have been characterized by abuses due in part to shortcomings in planning as well as to the vagaries of human nature. Through cartoons we can follow some of the problems which, if not controlled, could compromise the goals of the government for future development.

These problems are dealt with under the following categories:

1. Over-all drain on collective services due to cheating and non-cooperation of a social nature.
2. Personnel performance and management systems, including the nature of the bureaucratic structure.
3. Economic base issues: for example, those relating to unemployment and its impact; lack of cooperation among producing units; and adjustments in the foreign sector.

I. DRAIN ON COLLECTIVE SERVICES

Public Health

Adequate health care is one of China's priority objectives, but the system has been subjected to abuse.[1]

I.1

"Eating from the same big pot." (I.1)

一人 "有病"，全家吃药   李乃良

One member sick; whole family on free medication

---

[1] All college students, teachers and state employees, including retirees, qualify for free medical allowances, set at 30 yuan per capita in 1982. Actual cost to the state in 1979, however, was 40 yuan and in 1981 and 1982, the respective costs were 45 yuan and 50 yuan. The additional costs were due largely to "eating from the same big pot" — a term for indiscriminate use of centralized state funds. Some hospitals sold nutrients and other non-medical commodities as medicine. One hospital earned 52 per cent of its 1982 revenue in this way. In another instance of abuse, one cadre spent over 570 yuan from public funds in 1982 buying medicine which he gave to family members — he himself was never ill. (Jul. 13)

133

I.2

Abuse of health care.[1] (I.2)

医 院 饭 馆 化 *Hospital – Restaurant style* 徐振明

肉桂、参茸、虎骨酒……来啦

(Nurse bringing all kinds of goodies to patient)

---

[1] One report stated as follows: Patients with certain foot problems now get certain kinds of socks to cure and prevent foot tinea. Since being prescribed, and therefore free, the number of foot tinea patients has increased, as did the hospital income and employee bonuses. "As far as I know," the report continued, "some hospitals now prescribe 'medical toothpaste' in addition to 'medical socks'. If this trend is not stopped, there will probably be 'medical jackets' for skin disease, 'medical caps' for scalp problems, and 'medical trousers' for arthritis. If this happens, the 'big pot' will have become the 'big closet'." (Aug. 27)

A new system was introduced in 1983 whereby each hospital is allocated a set amount for each patient. If less is spent, the patient keeps the difference. If the limit is exceeded, the patient pays the difference. (Jul. 13)

Further abuse of the health system.
(I.3, I.4)

I.3

「合作」医疗（原载《北京晚报》）徐振明

One week sick leave

Treatment: therapeutic cooperation

I.4

堆说我没病！

Who said I am not sick?

文明缺乏症

Diagnosis – Rudeness

李洞滨

Restaurants are the initial targets of a new sanitation drive. (I.5, I.6, I.7)

I.5

Going to restaurant

I.6

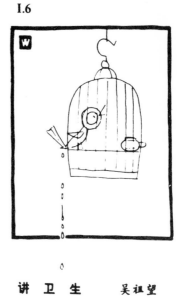

讲 卫 生　　吴祖望

Sanitary environment

I.7

人不留客地留客　　　　　阮 菘

Sticky-floor welcome

Stricter sanitary requirements are now being enforced in China. On July 1st, 1983, the first comprehensive food hygiene law consolidated previous measures. Standards are now set for food hygiene — additives, containers, packaging, manufacture, management and supervision.[1]

---

[1] The standards are being strictly enforced. By the end of the first week of their introduction, 89 state-run groceries, small restaurants and individual businesses were fined for unsanitary conditions. By the following week 26 food shops and producing factories were closed in Guangzhou "until unsanitary conditions are cleared up." (Jul. 8, 16)

I.8

Combined campaign: "Sanitation + Courtesy" (I.8, I.9)

Why look at me like that! Look at your menu.

——看我干什么？看菜单   姜振民

I.9

Sanitation first

如此讲卫生
Such sanitation

丁聪画   池北偶诗

搞卫生不卫生，
讲文明不文明。
你在吃饭他扫地，
尘土飞扬满餐厅。
一家方便百家愁，
饭菜肮脏地干净。
顾客花钱找罪受，
倒了胃口扫了兴。
如此饭馆实在杀风景！

Achieve clean and sanitary environment

Improve service

Be civil and polite

Such Sanitation (I.9)

Not sanitary when
   working on sanitation!
Not civil when
   bragging about civility.
I'm eating, she sweeping
   dust all around the dining hall.

One happy
   hundreds suffer
Food is filthy
   while dirt floor clean.
Customers pay to suffer
   lost appetite
   lost enthusiasm.

Such restaurant!
Deplorable.

I.10

Health standards cannot be maintained unless the people themselves accept these standards. (I.10)

——茶杯未消毒，当心得肝炎

——不要紧！我已有肝炎

潘文辉

I.11

——大家别忙了，今天不来检查卫生啦！

赵时铭

Irresponsible cadre conspires with irresponsible workers. (I.11)

Don't bother cleaning! Inspector won't come today.

The importance of example. (I.12)

I.12

翻到第一课，《人人小讲卫生》……

Turn to page 1. "Hygiene begins in childhood."

言 传 身 教 *Teaching by example* 叶建

An estimated 8 billion tons of water is wasted each year in China, much of it as the result of the abuse of collective resources.[1]

I.13

横竖不花钱

唐伯钧

Water free of charge

Household water waste. (I.13, I.14)

I.14

Baptize a wee bunch of onions
一棵小意的洗礼   吴祖望

[1] The shortage of water in 40 major cities is such that conservation is of strategic importance. "Some cities have had to ration water, and some factories have had to stop production from time to time in the dry seasons to ensure the supply for household use." (Oct. 8) Industrial use of water is about 80 per cent, but approximately 70 per cent is wasted. (Oct. 10) The waste on the residential side is such that a resident of Hong Kong on a visit to Nanching commented that "This is one of the merits of socialism" on seeing the extent of water wasted. (Je. 15) (China supplies water to Hong Kong.)

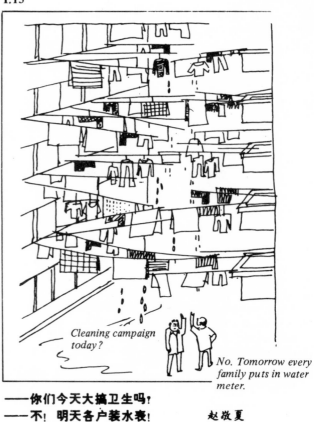

I.15

Individual meters are being introduced in cities as a means of reducing household consumption of water.[1] (I.15)

Cleaning campaign today?

No. Tomorrow every family puts in water meter.

——你们今天大搞卫生吗?
——不! 明天各户装水表!

赵敬夏

---

[1] The saving in water consumption has been considerable. In one building 42 families were paying 90 yuan per month for water, while the state subsidized its use at a cost of over 500 yuan each month. From 1979 to 1982, over 50,000 yuan were paid in subsidies to the water company. Each family now has a water meter. Subsidies are no longer necessary, and the water fee has dropped to 80 yuan per month. (June 25) Similarly, Beijing Optical factory realized savings when individual meters were installed for its 2,400 employees. The factory had been paying an average of 2,200 yuan per month to subsidize the fixed 300 yuan paid by each family. With the installation of meters, 50,000 tons of water was saved each month. (Nov. 16)

I.16

守株待鋸

*Waiting
under
the tree*

兰孝生

Reminder of wanton destruction of trees in the past.[1] (I.16)

There has been widespread destruction of trees over the years due to uncontrolled cutting for firewood, funeral sites, and building construction. Annual tree-planting drives have been stepped up since 1978 to correct this situation.

Restoration of trees is seen as part of the modernization programme in the country for aesthetic reasons but also for soil erosion control as well as planned industrial use. Modern cooking appliances, the outlawing of clan burial sites, and the development of new building materials have reduced the problem of wanton destruction of trees, but reminders of past waste are drawn to people's attention from time to time.

---

[1] The cartoon recalls the Chinese fable of the peasant and the hare. According to the story, a peasant was sitting under a tree one night when a rabbit rushed into the tree and broke its neck. The peasant dined on the rabbit and never worked again. Each day he sat under the tree waiting for another rabbit to come by to provide his dinner. The rabbit never came, the peasant died from hunger, and since then the trees have all been cut down. The rabbit in the cartoon mocks the peasant waiting with his saw for the young tree to mature in the same manner as the fabled peasant awaited his dinner.

I.17

Wasted electricity is a concern in the cities.[1] (I.17)

不 夜 城   孙泽良、韩 冬

Well lit city

Electricity is now distributed all across China but, as with other resources, its judicious use is necessary so that both industrial and residential demands can be met.

---

[1] The cartoon shows a peasant newly arrived in the city. Seeing the lights in the office building he happily rushes to get there on time. On arrival, he is astonished to find it closed and the electricity wasted.

Theft from public property in whatever form is a drain on the collective treasury. This is especially serious in a socialist economy where user fees are set at a minimal subsidized level. A number of situations are brought out in the cartoons below.

I.18

Cheating on train fares.[1] (I.18)

不是游戏   张新华

This is not playing the game

I.19

Cheating on bus fares.[2] (I.19)

Ticket purchasing

---

[1] Train attendant who has railway compartment filled with family and/or friends without tickets wards off inspector.

[2] Passengers should buy tickets and hand them to the ticket seller on leaving the bus. The tickets are then destroyed and put in a special container. Some passengers leave by the back door without purchasing tickets. Inspectors make spot checks on the buses and impose fines on anyone found without a ticket.

I.20

拣 票 员 *Ticket picking* 常 进

Cheating on expense account.[1]
(I.20)

I.21

*Conference gist
and local produce
all here*

交 差 *Back from assignment* 杨成志
——会议精神、土特产都在这里

Gifts as a bribe for the supervisor.[2]
(I.21)

---

[1] Cadre on out-of-town assignment picks up discarded tickets which he will submit as part of his expense account. These tickets should have been placed in a special container. (See note 2, p. 143).

[2] The implications are that some special privilege was attached to the assignment.

I.22

Delegation of "Learning from the Pine Tree's Spirit"

Pleasure trip on pretext of study mission (I.22)

"下一日程是学习黄山松!" 韦启美

Next trip is to learn from the pine trees at Yellow Mountain[1]

---

[1] The pine tree is the symbol of endurance and firmness. The delegation has returned "full of inspiration" and is planning their trip to the next picturesque city. The public funds spent on unnecessary trips is of no concern to them.

I.23

步话机（原载《工人日报》） 梅逢春

Cigarette radio

Leading cadres at times used "their offices to acquire any goods desired — from electric fans to towels, soap and batteries."[1] (Aug. 17) (I.23, I.24)

I.24

"以 厂 为 家" *Factory is my home*[2] 卫庆前

---

[1] Such practices are severely punished. In 1983, for example, two officials from one province were given prison terms of 20 and 18 years respectively for buying smuggled goods which were then re-sold at a profit to the state store of which one was a director. The other arranged for forged or altered customs receipts. (Aug. 17)

[2] All taken from factory supplies.

Another aspect to the theft of state goods is the complacency with which others accept it.

I.25

Somebody's philosophy

I.26

稻草人看家   孙以增

Scarecrow factory security guard

The philosophy of "minding one's own business in order to lead an easy life means the sacrifice of the Party's principles and the interests of the people." (Aug. 17) (I.25, I.26, I.27)

I.27

石 狮 子 *Stone lion sitting at gate* 姜振民

Private and cooperative output are encouraged as an important supplement to state output. From this point of view, theft from private property is akin to theft from the state.

I.28[1]

Help yourself with the fruit

Some peasants, workers and professionals who have increased their productivity under the incentives of the Responsibility Movement[2] become the prey of others — whether incited by jealousy, laziness or greed. (I.28)

---

[1] Award-winning family blackmailed by neighbours.

[2] See Section A, p. 19.

Another version of theft from private property. (I.29)

I.29

吃庄稼的老虎 *Tiger after prey* 韦启美

J. PERSONNEL AND MANAGEMENT

The Bureaucracy

When the People's Republic was established in 1949, decentralized administrative units were introduced to implement policies set at the national level. In the process, the number of cadres multiplied considerably. The performance of the cadres was subjected to constant scrutiny by those above and below, and anyone found wanting was subjected to criticism. Obligatory political study helped to keep in focus the principle of dedication to duty by cadres, workers and peasants.

Since 1978, cadres have been given a significant amount of autonomy compatible with the spirit of the Responsibility Movement. At the same time, productivity has become a criterion of efficiency, with a de-emphasis on political philosophy or family background, factors which were previously of primary importance. These changes have brought to the fore unsatisfactory levels of performance — whether due to indifference, incompetence, arbitrary and unreasonable decisions, and/or the desire for self-aggrandizement. Some of these aspects are brought out in the cartoons which follow.[1]

As a result of the Iron Rice Bowl and a lack of efficient rationalization of the labour force in the past, there is a problem of superfluous cadres. (J.1)

J.1

五哥放羊 *Five shepherds, one sheep* 王力加

---

[1] Top level cadres have been included in the over-all assessments. The approach taken is that "the key lies with the leaders. It is no use calling a meeting only to give instructions. With the bureaucracy, a problem remains a problem." (Jul. 28) Therefore all levels of cadres are affected by the re-organization measures subsequently introduced.

J.2[1]

以十当一

Ten to one

通子

Work multiplies proportionate to the number of hands available. (J.2, J.3)

J.3

Guidelines from supervisor

+*guidelines to enforce guidelines from supervisor*

+*guidelines to enforce guidelines to enforce . . .*

滚雪球　　高世谅

Snowballing

---

[1]   Ten clerks to sell one shirt.

During the period of the Cultural Revolution, the practice of self-criticism as well as that of yielding to the criticism of others was carried to excess. In some cases, key cadres were "criticized" to death. Partly for this reason, but also to reflect the new liberalism in China today, criticism as a means of rectification has been de-emphasized and, when used, is often treated lightly by some cadres.

J.5

Criticism of director — extinguisher necessary

"They do not heed criticism, and have even resorted to feudal attitudes where they see themselves above reproach." (Jul. 15) (J.5)

Some cadres "reverse" criticism to the disadvantage or embarrassment of those who complained. (J.4)

J.4

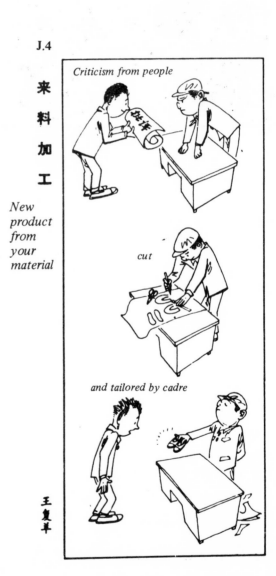

New product from your material

Criticism from people

cut

and tailored by cadre

Some cadres display a spirit of superiority, disregarding the slogan "Serve the people."[1] (J.6)

J.6

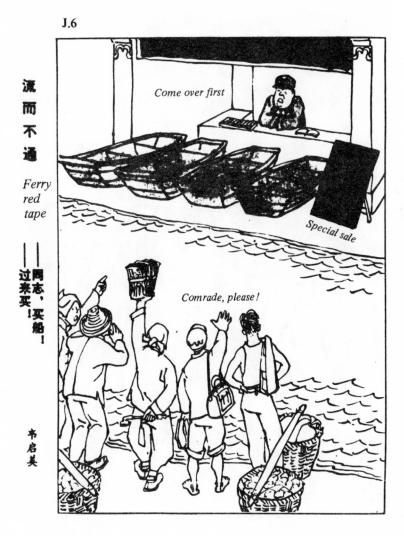

J.7

菜 谱

Item 12: cabbage 50 cents
Item 13: carrots 50 cents

"Non-cadre" menu.[1] (J.7)

厂长不在食堂吃饭了　　　　　白维纯

The boss doesn't eat here anymore

J.8

「嗯，这面镜子不错」

韦启美

Hum . . . not bad, this mirror

Because of tradition, people expect cadres to seem distinct from workers and peasants, official policy notwithstanding.[2] (J.8)

---

[1] At a certain restaurant, the menu lacks variety and prices are 10 times higher than they should be. Should the "boss" decide to eat there, the menu would become attractive and the prices reasonable. (This is a situation frequently complained of in the press.)

[2] A writer in **China Daily** stated that "official airs we often see today have not appeared suddenly. They have their historical background, and therefore will not disappear so easily." Hierarchical status was rigid in ancient China. The Confucian classic **Gong Yang Zhuan** on the history of the Spring and Autumn Period (722 to 481 B.C.) stated: "The horses of the Son of Heaven, i.e., the Emperor, are called dragons, their height being over seven feet. The horses of the marquis are over six feet tall, and those of senior officials are called colts, being over five feet in height." (Nov. 12)

The following excerpt points to the expected behaviour of cadres today. "A leading comrade of the Central Committee Discipline Commission, visiting a certain guest house, aroused the suspicions of a desk clerk. The clerk thought the newcomer an imposter because he did not look like a high-ranking cadre from one of the Party's top organizations. He had neither bodyguards nor attendants. He did not have the 'air' of a high official . . . . (The clerk) had been dutiful and observant. He was used to cadres of high, middle and low rank, who all have 'airs'. They have special bearing and talk differently. Sometimes, the lower the rank, the more 'airs' a cadre puts on." (Nov. 11)

J.9

The tendency of looking up to those in higher positions has laid the basis for bribes and abuse of power in a variety of forms and at varying levels. (J.9, J.10)

病从口人   王立人

Sickness because of greed

(Bribe is the bacteria)

J.10

进 贡   *Unchanged scenario*   冯笪 杨德林

155

'Corrupt cadres'. (J.11, J.12, J.13)

J.12

大 实 话　　　　　　　洁 秋

(Best parts left by back door)

J.11

(a) Fear of accusation 冯春生
(b) "Another gift"

J.13

家里事单位办　单位事家里办

周正安（沈阳）

Mix-up of domestic and business affairs

Some cadres have to be bribed before they look to their responsibilities.[1] (J.14)

J.14

Too many dishes

Main dish last!

---

[1] In a case reported in 1983, for example, a group of five electricians were offered cigarettes and tea when they went to install lines for a commune. However they went on a "go slow" routine until served chicken and duck as special treats. They also "felt neglected if the commune leader did not remain with them all the time." (Aug. 3)

In another situation, a number of plumbers with a certain engineering company extorted payments for speedy repairs to pipes and taps in homes. If the work was finished more quickly than they planned after the initial supplementary payment, they would refuse to leave until given an additional payment. After complaints were made against them, they were ordered to refund the payments. (Aug. 11)

J.15

CHINA DAILY
Jul. 28, 1983

Unacceptable practices of senior cadres are often blamed on women.[1] (J.15)

"Clean cadres" repulse temptation. (J.16)

J.16

---

[1] See p. 88.

Among the cadres who hinder progress are those who regard their jobs as "tools" for personal gain. (J.17)

J.17

装饰壁画   *High-flying ambitions*

J.18

Some cadres see their jobs as "arm-chairs" for ease and comfort.[1]
(J.18, J.19)

公 事 电 话 *Office workers*　　刘渔存

J.19

静物画展

李之久

Still life

---

[1] A tourist reportedly expressed surprise at a cadre's complacency while a 500-room hotel, completed 18 months ago, remained unoccupied. The cadre's response was to this effect: "Why should I care? I do not fear dismissal; my salary is low — let someone else worry about the problem." (Jul. 9)

J.20

The "big mouth" productively ineffective type of cadre is self-centred, blind and deaf to issues and ideas around hum. (J.20)

Rank and file —
big mouth without
eyes and ears

J.21

Country and people — none of my business

什么国家大事与我无关!

吃
玩
唱

不问

Shut up
in myself

不闻

Deaf to critics

发育不全 *Deformed infant* 郝玉华

Others see but are without ears or mouth — shut up in themselves. (J.21)

Some cadres, instead of using the autonomy offered under the Responsibility Movement to increase productivity, resort to amassing titles for self-aggrandizement. (J.22, J.23)

J.22

一个萝卜几个坑

王复羊

Positions held concurrently

One carrot — several holes

J.23[1]

I'm the director, why can't I have the title of engineer?

---

[1] "Previously many administrators who had no professional training took pride in being uneducated." (Aug. 10) This was up to 1976 when being educated placed one in the undesirable "intellectual" category. "Now they have suddenly wanted to become engineers, technicians, and economists." (Jul. 19)

The multiplicity of roles leads to
inefficiency and frustration on the
part of the title-holder, and complaints by qualified by-standers.[1]
(J.24)

J.24

吃 不 消   *Too heavy weights*[2]   孙以增

---

[1] The Party secretary and vice principal of one institution
was also professor, special researcher, director, standing
committee member, chairman, and vice-chairman. In and
out of the institution he held over a dozen titles. "If a
professor does not teach and a director does not direct,
but (rather) take part in meetings and get-togethers most
of the time, what sort of social environment will they
create?" asks **China Daily**. (Jul. 9)

[2] Weights translate: chairman, president, director, honorary
president, advisor, executive director, artistic counsel,
. . . meetings, reports, interviews, etc.

From 1949 to 1976 attendance at meetings was encouraged and expected as part of the concept of total national involvement. Decision-making committees at the local level represented workers, cadres, the inexperienced, the retired, young and old, men and women, One off-shoot was the loss of innumerable working hours due to time off for meetings. To reduce this loss, meetings have been de-emphasized.

> Meetings have lost their effectiveness as a symbol of participatory decision-making. (J.25)

J.25

A meeting of representatives. China Daily, Sept. 19, 1983
by Ge Jian
reprinted from Dazhong Ribao

J.26

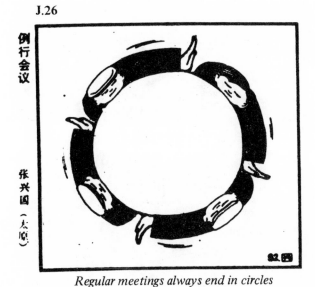

例行会议

张兴国（太原）

Regular meetings always end in circles

Decline in the significance of meetings.[1] (J.26, J.27)

J.27

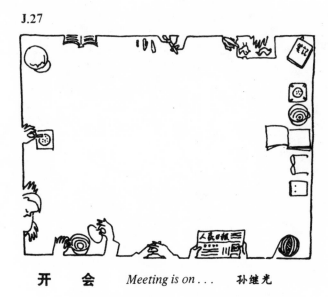

开　会　　*Meeting is on . . .*　孙继光

(Everybody busy at something else)

---

[1] Workers have complained that "their congresses have become only nominal organs of power, like chopped onions scattered on a dish just for seasoning and looks." The bureaucracy is so entrenched, that at times "resolutions are no more than repetitions of the Party Committee of factory administrators' decisions," stated one worker. "In just one day at one congress, the factory leaders gave five reports and all resolutions were adopted. Workers said they had sent their representatives to the congress only to raise their hands." (Sept. 3)

The ineffectiveness of their express-ed opinions has brought about a disinterest by delegates in meet-ings.[1] (J.28, J. 29)

J.28

Listening to the report

J.29   *(a)*   *(b)*

Not doing what was told
(a: indifference; b: adjournment)

---

[1] "Leaders at one factory drew up a plan for distributing housing and sent it to the congress for approval. Most workers' representatives refused to endorse it. The leaders then decided that it could be passed by acclamation." (Sept. 3)

In 1978 it was recognized that individual initiative had to be stimulated in order to increase productivity. The bonus system was therefore expanded, but the result has not been entirely satisfactory, as shown in cartoons J.30 to J.36.

J.30

Initiative has to be stimulated. (J. (J.30)

不自动的 "售货机"　　洪顺海

Non-automatic vending machine

J.31

In general, only a few workers qualify for an honest bonus. Those that do stand out as model workers and at times become objects of envy among their co-workers. (J.31)

Who said I have a poker face?　　*(Only one got a bonus)*

"谁说我没笑脸"　　　　哈笑（沈阳）

J.32

Model worker — an object of
envy.[1] (J.32)

近朱者赤

哈
笑

Admirers blushing

A problem faced by managers is how to maintain staff morale when levels of productivity are close
to each other, but one or two members are to be singled out for the bonus.

J.33

多劳多得 *Overpaid*[2] 陈跛子

Accusations of favouritism, real or
imagined, surface. (J.33)

---

[1] Red face, red neck and red eyes are represented in the cartoon, symbolizing envy.

[2] Painter rewarded for adding feet to snake.

J.34

「新年到放鞭炮」

徐振明

New Year's firecrackers (symbolizing public assets on bonus at year end)

To avoid charges of favouritism, some managers give bonuses to the entire staff as long as productivity is up. (J.34)

J.35

"吃老本"　　　仲维国（沈阳）

Eating my bonus away

One drawback with giving bonuses to the entire staff is that a worker can nonchalantly "eat his bonus away" with the penalty distributed across his unit. He will himself still be ahead as long as the others in his unit have brought about an over-all increase. (J.35)

Some enterprises make money out of "backwardness", i.e., by setting low quotas and showing an increase in profits for distribution as a bonus.[1]

Others simply give bonuses indiscriminately. (J.36)

J.36

为 "向钱看" 者造像 *A portrait of looking forward* 刘 雍

(always towards the stack of money)

---

[1] One firm, following this method, quadrupled bonuses to employees in three months in 1983, although sales and profits were only 24 per cent and 30 per cent higher than in 1982. (July 7)

Rejuvenation calls for changes in attitudes.

Cadres are exhorted to participate,
to set examples and not simply
issue orders. (J.37)

J.37

Three shouts are not worth one act

The result of incompetence – management by dissimulation.[1] (J.38, J.39)

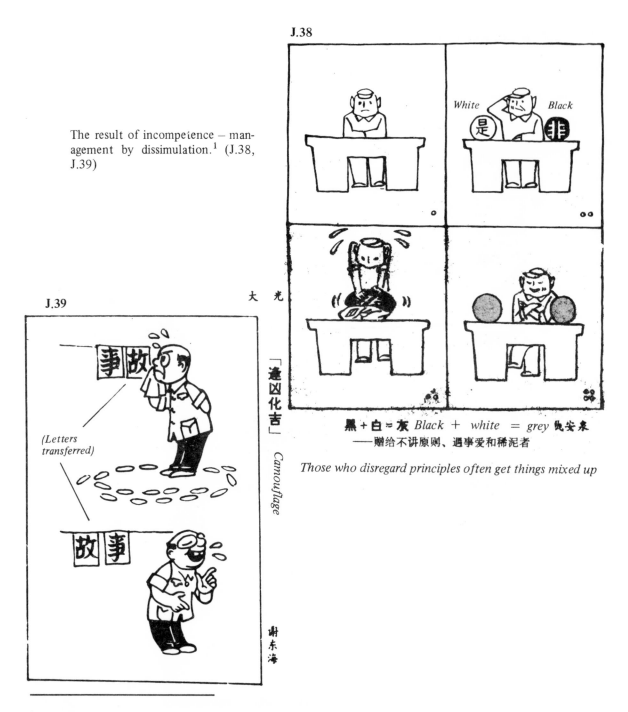

J.38

White 是 Black 非

黑 + 白 = 灰 Black + white = grey
——赠给不讲原则、遇事爱和稀泥者

逢凶化吉 Camouflage

大光

Those who disregard principles often get things mixed up

J.39

事故 故事

(Letters transferred)

谢东海

---

[1] A tendency of some cadres is to present a situation in a favourable light when they have difficulty solving it, thus emulating Mao Zedung's exhortation to "turn adversity to advantage." Mao's intent was not that problems should not be solved, but that they should be seen as an opportunity to correct and improve areas of weakness.

J.40

幌 子

张文石

*Body protection
(research plan)*

Some cadres launch "research projects" instead of immediately attacking a problem. (J.40)

Their contribution to the modernization drive can be likened to the impossible task of "piercing a stone with drops of water." (J.41)

J.41

滴水穿石法

*Method of
piercing the
stone with
drops of
water*

急待解决的问题

Urgent problems

孙中道

173

J.42

The level of research by some cadres is akin to "inventing the conversion of corn to popcorn."[1] (J.42)

爆 米 花 *Popcorn* 王恩华

(corn symbolizes achievement on report card)

---

[1] Example of non-innovative research. The "inventor" receives great satisfaction from what to him was a complicated experiment – converting corn to popcorn. State Incentive Awards introduced in 1963 but discontinued during the Cultural Revolution, have been restored to encourage innovative progress in a variety of fields such as agriculture, industry, and medicine. Four hundred and eighteen awards were given in 1982. (Jul. 16)

Steps are being taken to facilitate the entry of younger cadres into positions of leadership.[1]

J.43

We'll grow old together

白首偕老   肖 洛

（有感于某些商品的式样）

Some product designs

Unproductive "researchers".
(J.43, J.44)

J.44

*Laurel and Hardy: sitting tight in the name
of doing research*

哼哈二将   八字胡华研武

In 1982 the average retirement age of junior cadres was set at 60 for men and 50 for women. Senior cadres were allowed to stay longer, although 470,000 veteran cadres retired when the new system was introduced in 1982. This represented one-sixth of Party and government leaders and of office workers who took office in 1949 when the People's Republic was established. (Jul. 18)

J.45

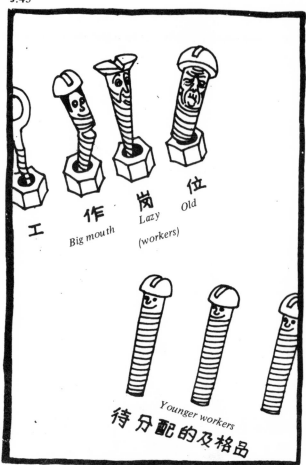

Conception of older cadres. (J.45, J.46)

Consistency   (Dancing to unchanged tune)

J.46

With rejuvenation, there is the encouragement of new talent.

Condemnation of those who discourage initiative. (J.47)

A cadre is like a bus driver "who, when reaching the ripe age of 60, may have bad eyesight, and may endanger the lives of his passengers . . . ." After a "certain age, he should sit by the side of a new driver and teach the younger man how to do his job properly." (Jul. 11)

An older cadre should "pass on his load with joy." (J.48)

J.47

Expert critic

J.48

扶上马　送一程　　王大充

The "send-off"

The dynamism of youth versus the stability of age. (J.49)

J.49

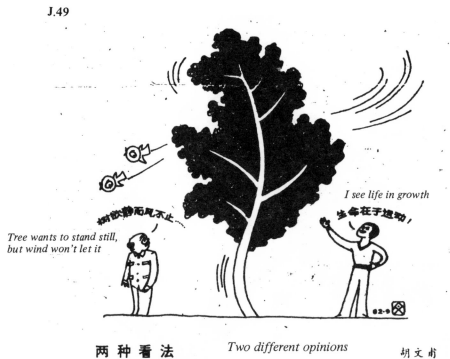

两 种 看 法 *Two different opinions*

"Like waves rolling down the Yangtze River," a new generation of cadres is gradually succeeding its elders in central and provincial leading organizations, following the directives of the central government. (Je. 26)

The movement is viewed with caution, lest emerging bright cadres be over-burdened with too many responsibilities and expectations. (J.50)

J.50

有碍于飞翔　刘 牵

Hindrance to flying high

Overpraise

"An army competently led is apt to win and (similarly) a well managed enterprise can produce better results." With this as a premise, an intensified management upgrading programme is being pursued, at the end of which, the majority of inefficient managers will be removed.[1]

"Empty belly" typifies an inefficient manager unable to develop a plan of action when faced with a problem. (J.51)

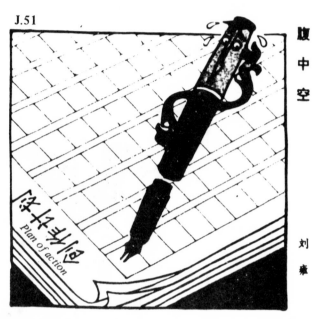

Empty belly

---

[1] "Over 70 per cent of the present management staff do not have an education greater than the level of middle junior school, while over 70 per cent of the technical workers are below the level of junior grade three." (Nov. 19)

There are plans for all directors, managers and deputy-managers of state-run enterprises to be tested on material relating to "principles and policies for economic construction and basic knowledge of business management." (Aug. 8) By the end of 1984, it is proposed to have 1,000 tests completed, and only those who pass will be allowed to keep their jobs. (Aug. 10) Training programmes in preparation for the tests are being conducted in key centres, many with the aid of foreign experts in management systems.

Some cadres hide from problem issues because of their inadequacy. (J.52, J.53)

J.52

捉迷藏

*Hide
and seek*

袁国镇

Problems

Leave the problems to others

J.53

勇挑重担

On leave

王益生

Leave the problems to others

Superfluous organizations and a resulting complexity of red tape[1] and inefficiency emerge as problems which are being addressed under management reorganization.

"Handicapped" by overlapping organizations. (J.54)

J.54

Handicapped

---

[1] A railway employee, for example, wrote to a newspaper about inadequate security in his section. His letter was immediately passed on to the Provincial Party Committee, then sent to the railway bureau which channelled it to a sub-bureau for action. After nine months the letter was returned to the desk of the original writer without any remedial action having been taken. The writer then updated the letter and rechannelled it, hoping for some action before it came back to his desk. In the meantime he wrote to the newspaper complaining about the bureaucratic "jungle". (Jul. 9)

Structured red tape.[1] (J.56)

J.55

J.56

有感于精简机构　　白维虎

Superfluous organizations

排队有术 *Unique way to queue* 孙泽良

---

[1]　Note how the last person in the queue copes with the structure.

Reorganization has taken place along two fronts: one discarding the unitary managerial system,[1] which is seen as "too rigid and stereotyped"; and the other, making structural changes to provide more coordinated leadership.[2]

Lack of coordination. (J.57)

J.57

Separated by their wall

---

[1] Refers to the same pattern indiscriminately applied to administrative, technical, scientific and cultural workers. (Nov. 2)

[2] The Petro-Chemical Corporation affords an example of structural changes. "In 1979, thirty-nine related enterprises, scattered under different levels of governments across the country, were amalgamated under three ministries concentrating on oil, chemicals and textiles. However, leadership was provided at two or three different levels, that is, many-headed leadership by the central government, the provinces and the cities. This resulted in lack of coordination and management, with different targets for production, value, variety and quality. Marketing channels were confused, exchange of technical personnel blocked, and there was no unified planning for research and development. Profits in the industry were high, but they were mostly caused through the pricing factors and did not accurately reflect actual economic results." (Aug. 2)

In 1983, the petro-chemical firms were consolidated under one corporation providing for rationalization of production and productivity, as well as flexibility in personnel policies based on performance. **(Ibid.)**

Coordinated leadership required.[1]
(J.58)

J.58

割席而坐 *Each his own seat* 江有生

---

1 An example of the need for coordinated leadership is offered by the following case: "The . . . Bank notified a mirror-making factory that in future it must use aluminium instead of silver. But the city financial department refused to allocate funds for the change-over. The city economic commission joined forces with the bank to stop supplying the factory with silver nitrate. Soon the factory was forced to stop production. It was only after the provincial authorities heard of the matter that the factory started the renovation programme." (Nov. 29)

   Periodic checks are planned to "decide promotion, demotion and dismissal of cadres," but there are doubts that this can be left completely in the hands of cadres themselves. The masses are therefore invited to recommend cadres for appointment, but also to be involved in steps to "test, supervise, promote and demote cadres" who, through their abilities or actions, compromise in any way the principles of the state and the modernization process.[1] (Nov. 2)

J.59

Some cadres are unwilling to criticize themselves or each other. (J.59)

Chess: criticism vs self-criticism

观棋不语

By-standers shut up

支南平

---

[1] For example, under the reorganization programme, underway in 1983, a factory worker informed the Vice Minister of the State Economic Commission that some enterprises, approved as "reorganized enterprises" by the Commission, "may not really be up to standard." Some, it was stated, were "far below" the State's standards. "In most cases, the 'examination group' " yielded to personal favours in approving the enterprises. As a result of this complaint, reported in the **Workers' Daily** (*Gongren Ribao*), workers were urged to follow the example of the complaining worker and monitor the behaviour of their cadres. (Nov. 29)

"Party cadres in particular should know that the working class and the masses are the masters of the country, and they, as cadres, are servants of the people." (Dec. 30)

J.60

Workers are called on to protect the collective interest. (J.60, J.61)

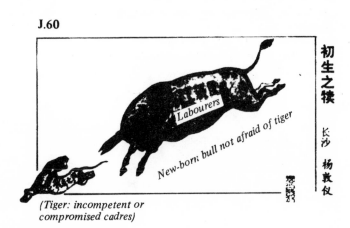

初生之犊 长沙 杨敢仪

New-born bull not afraid of tiger

(Tiger: incompetent or compromised cadres)

J.61

Tough guy

硬功夫　　*Anti-corruption*　　王复羊

187

K. SELECTED ECONOMIC BASE ISSUES

All the issues in this book have an economic base in the sense that cultural patterns and aspirations, economic behaviour, standards of living and changes in social relationships are influenced by the type of economic environment — affluent or poor, stimulating or depressing, opportunities for horizontal or vertical mobility.

In this section some key economic issues are singled out within the limits of the cartoons covered.

These reflect concerns raised by the Chinese themselves during the period, namely:

— Illegal pedlars;
— Abuse of the spirit of the Responsibility Movement;
— Lack of cooperation and the extent of competitive advertising;
— Quality control;
— Foreign economic relations.

Illegal Pedlars

In one district of Shanghai, unlicensed pedlars have been removed or fined, and itinerants ordered to return to their native towns. (K.1)[1] (June 22)

Individually-run businesses have been promoted since 1979 in order to cope with the rising unemployment, to encourage private initiative and to supplement output from state-run enterprises. Most of these "businesses" consist of pedlars whose number has multiplied in both urban and rural areas. Many cities have introduced curbs on these itinerants, most of whom are unlicensed. In 1983 consideration was being given to issuing licenses only to jobless youth, urban unemployed in financial difficulties and retirees. (Jul. 1)

K.1

古 城 新 墙   法 生

有些地区搞封建主义经济封锁，本位主义的
经营作风。   *Old city; new walls*

(to ward off out of town pedlars)

---

[1] Another interpretation of this cartoon is as a criticism of a monopoly tendency by established enterprises which impose restraints, making it difficult for competitors to enter the field. (Information supplied by visiting scholars.)

Inspection of 2,407 collectively-run enterprises in one province in 1983 showed that 1,028 had evaded taxation by more than 30 methods. (Nov. 19) (K.2)

K.2

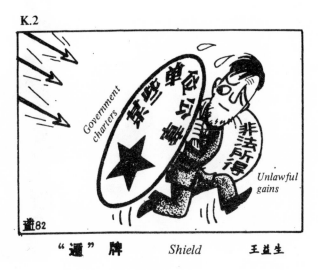

Government charters

Unlawful gains

"通" 牌　　*Shield*　　王益生

The spirit of the Responsibility Movement entails encouraging individual initiative, on the premise that there will be a positive communal spin-off. However, institutional manipulation presents a problem as evidenced by the extent of tax evasion.[1]

---

[1] The Ministry of Finance cites the following factors as contributing to tax evasion:
- Some local governments have instructed agencies to reduce or exempt business tax in disregard of State tax regulations;
- Sometimes tax collectors are barred from entering businesses or consulting necessary data;
- Some hostile people even attack tax collectors, but are not taken seriously by the justice system;
- Businesses have developed a variety of ways to evade taxes. (Nov. 19)

Peasants also cheat the Treasury. Some when selling goods to the State have been known to "mix good fruits with rotten ones; put stones in baskets; sell in great quantities the kind of grain and vegetables that have a low price on the open market and retain those which sell at high prices out of season." (Nov. 14)

Competitive production practices
led to "overlapping brands". (K.3)

K.3

重叠牌挂钟　青岛　韩 冰

Clock of overlapping brand

Following the widespread promotion of economic development introduced in 1978, shortages developed in many industries. The response was a competitive rush to build factories for the commodities in short supply. This created a build-up of surpluses in neighbouring communities and multiplicity of overlapping brands.[1]

---

[1] Another impact was a competitive demand for limited resources, so that material shortages developed and some factories had to cease production. The result was redundant factories in some places and surplus output in others.

An example of a redundant factory is the window factory in one commune that in 1982 spent 4 million yuan on expansion. In December 1983 it was still waiting for raw materials to start operations. This is one of a number of factories which responded to the rapid demand for steel doors following a 1979 construction boom. Instead of a planned output, 150 window factories were established in three neighbouring counties although there was not enough rolled steel to meet their demands. This factory survived the forced closings, but proceeded with an unauthorized expansion programme. (**Beijing Review,** Dec. 12, 1983)

Along with problems of surplus output and materials flow resulting from the establishment of unauthorized firms,[1] there is an increasing pressure on State firms to show profits. Many enterprises have therefore turned to active promotion of their products.

K.4

Active product promotion. (K.4)

借
光

*Borrow a favour
from a street light*

张
兴
升

*(Advertised goods: peanuts, candies, clock,
eyeglasses, T-shirts, rice pot, snacks, toiletries)*

[1] In 1980, State factories increased output of bicycles, sewing machines and wrist watches to meet the surge in demand which accompanied improved economic conditions. At the same time, provincial departments and local governments also set up factories outside the State plan. However, a surplus developed when many factories were unable to sell their output following a consumer shift to washing machines, refrigerators and electric fans.

The production of batteries shows a similar pattern. It is estimated that over-production will cost China 150 million yuan by the end of 1984. In 1983 there were 210 specialized factories with an annual output of 5 billion, whereas the national market could only absorb 3.6 billion. The rest would be scrapped. (Nov. 9)

There are so many unauthorized commune and local government factories producing soap, that it would take three years for the projected 1983 surplus to be used. In July 1983 the People's Bank therefore recommended that factories not be allowed to increase output, and that the local factories be closed. (Jul. 14)

"False front" advertising. (K.5)

K.5

I'm not old

不服老　　*Advertising mask*　　朱长清

"Drum" advertising for insignificant product. (K.6)

K.6

上海外滩小景

Scene from the Buod in Shanghai

At a national conference in July 1983, delegates from 20 major cities were asked to "strengthen their work on advertisement inspection and to punish those who are found to have offered false information in their advertisements to draw customers."[2] (Aug. 10)

---

[1] The Buod is a strip in Shanghai along the Whampoo River with the best seafood restaurants.

[2] In 1982, over 150 million yuan were spent on advertising. This represented an increase of 20 per cent over that spent in 1981.

Boosting products of little value.
(K.7)

K.7

Advertisements by entrepreneurs for their products

Some enterprises as a profit-generating device, sacrifice quality in pursuit of quantity.

K.8

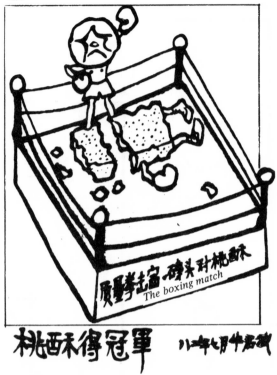

Poor quality products.[1] (K.8)

桃酥得冠軍　八一年七月牛启武

The cake shatters the brick

At the National People's Conference in June 1983, it was pointed out that increasing production at the sacrifice of quality, variety and cost-efficiency served only statistical and political purposes. On the other hand, the negative impact included stock-piling, slim revenues, poor commodity supplies, and jeopardizing the country's efforts to hold its own in international markets.[2]

---

[1] Poor quality nut cake is hard enough to shatter a brick.

[2] For the period 1980–1982, losses to the State from over-stocking due to poor quality were estimated at 12 billion yuan. (Nov. 14)

Twenty per cent of the problems in quality control for China's 400,000 industries might be due to laxity on the part of cadres or workmen, but a larger proportion re-flects low standards. (Nov. 19) In general, problems arise from "low production and poor management; most, especially in light industries, use machines 40 to 50 years old; the standard of products are 20 years behind those of developed countries, but energy consumption is great-er; the waste of manpower, money and raw materials is staggering; (and) the large number of unskilled workers." (Oct. 22)

Quality according to destination. (K.9)

K.9

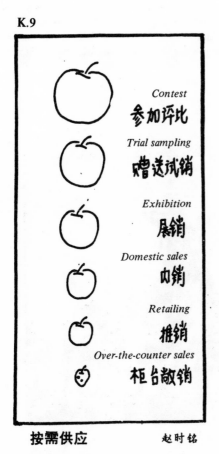

Contest
参加评比

Trial sampling
赠送试销

Exhibition
展销

Domestic sales
内销

Retailing
推销

Over-the-counter sales
柜台敞销

按需供应   赵时铭

Supply according to demand

Disregard of standards. (K.10)

K.10

产品规格"展"？   孟石初

Same measurement – product difference according to factory

Quality control associations are being established across the country, and are regarded as vital to the economy. (Oct. 22) They supplement short training quality-control courses now being offered.[1]

Tangible progress has been identified. Harbin Tool Factory, for example, has installed machines for checking quality and its products are now rated "second only to those made in Sweden and are better than similar British, Japanese and Soviet blades." The export market has been responsive and 25 per cent of the factory's tools were sold in over 30 countries in 1983. (Aug. 2)

---

[1] In 1983, between January and November, 271,220 such associations were established with a membership of 4 million. In the same period, 56,273 training courses were attended by 6.5 million workers and staff. (Nov. 4)

Since 1976, China has increasingly promoted foreign involvement in its economic development plans, as opposed to the previous policy of isolation based on the principle of self-reliance. At first, until 1981, over-enthusiasm to accelerate the pace of development led to indiscriminate signing of contracts with foreign enterprises and governments. These later presented a wide range of problems in areas such as foreign exchange shortage, bottlenecks from lack of project coordination, the absence of support bases for material flow, inappropriate and competing technology. Most of these contracts have been renegotiated, but some problems remaining from their impact are evident in the following cartoons.

K.11

Outdated foreign goods arriving from "friendly" countries. (K.11)

"丝绸之路" 遗风   韦启美

The "Silk Route"[1] legacy
(Newly arrived products of the 1950s)

---

[1] The Silk Road was the only route used for trade and exchange between ancient China and foreign countries. (Aug. 2; **Beijing Review**, Oct. 31, 1983)

K.12

"Undue stress was put on complete
plants to the neglect of key equipment needed by existing enterprises.
. . . Imports were duplicated with
inadequate assimilation."[1] (K.12)

钻木取火　　*Fire-making*　梅逢春

(Imported equipment to match obsolete domestic industries)

---

[1] For example, a certain fuel pump factory in Beijing was started in 1972 but was still idle at the end of 1983, unable to
meet minimum standards. Wages since 1980 were being met from capital construction funds. In the meantime, a large-
scale extension had been carried out with imported parts while "most of its 2,300 imported pieces of equipment had been
lying idle all along and some have become useless because of heavy rust." (Nov. 22)

K.13

"Killing the domestic electronics industry with foreign imports."[1] (K.13)

Blocking your own driveway

---

[1] China's current policy with regard to this industry was expressed by the Minister of Electronics Industry as follows: "In recent months we have been considering what strategy and technological policies to adopt in our development plan for the next 10 to 20 years . . . . If our decision and judgment are correct, we'll make a great effort to speed up the development of our electronics industry . . . . Electronics technology elsewhere in the world is advancing by leaps and bounds. This is a challenge as well as an opportunity. We should borrow from their experience and skip some of the stages of development. In this way we can adopt directly new technical achievements and develop more speedily." (Feb. 17, 1984)

The textile industry is one of the major contributors to foreign exchange.

China is achieving diversity in its export base to reduce its dependence on textiles, but in the meantime, has been able to defend the market against attempts by importers to impose any significant reduction in sales.[1]

There is keen competition among firms for export sales. (K.14)

K.14

Export bargaining – Piece goods

While effecting corrective measures internally, China will and can defend its external trade relations on the principle of mutual benefit and on terms it considers acceptable. Expansion of trade and technological cooperation will take place as long as these contribute to the improvement of China's economic performance but according to the State Councillor Zheng Jingfu, the relationships "will be adversely affected if policies of restriction or discrimination are pursued against China in trade and technical exchange, no matter what fine words may be said." (Oct. 15)

---

[1] When a dispute over quotas developed with the United States in January 1983, for example, China halted purchases of soybeans, cotton and synthetic fibres and reduced its purchases of wheat, bringing about a 73 per cent reduction in its intake of agricultural exports from the United States in nine months. The over-all reduction in United States' exports to China was 40 per cent, resulting in a United States-China trade deficit of $246 million compared to a surplus of $652.2 million in favour cf the United States the previous year. (**The Globe and Mail**, Nov. 28, 1983) A new textile agreement was signed in August 1983 on terms acceptable to China.

CONCLUSION

Readers on reflection, will find that there is nothing uniquely Chinese about the fundamental messages expressed in the cartoons in this book. The issues are universally applicable, and countries far more economically developed than China present parallel cases. From this point of view, then, the cartoons serve to inform those who are unsure of their conception of China, that its people are just people like all others.

It is worth noting also that in the hundreds of cartoons reproduced here, a picture of creeping affluence has emerged surrounded by questioning acceptance of manifestations linked to this affluence. By focussing on areas of doubt — areas of disturbing concern in their environment — and exposing these to the public at large, the Chinese have displayed a singular quality. Other countries may analyze their own faults, areas of weakness and uncertainties, but few, if any, have taken steps to expose them internally and externally. In China today there is a definite effort to communicate problems, concerns and achievements in such a way that the majority of the population is informed, and to expose to outsiders discussions of these internal issues. To foreigners who comment on this openness, the Chinese reply: "We do not hide our errors and defects. We make them public, because we have faith and strength to correct them in a set time."

These cartoons have revealed some of China's priorities between 1982 and 1983. Since then, there has been a shift in focus from moral concerns to economic modernization. This book will have paved the way for a better understanding of the dynamic changes continually evidenced in a country of over a billion people bent on accelerated modernization but concerned about the attending social and cultural fallout.